Time Passages

By Robert Burtt & Bill Main

"The key to unlocking the door to our future opens with a journey into the past."

Second Printing

JANUARY 1977

President Carter enjoys the Inaugural Parade with wife Rosalynn, daughter Amy and VP Walter Mondale.

Sunday	Monday	Tuesday	Wednesday	Thursday	Friday	Saturday
		O.J. Simpson stars as an African tribesman who gives a young "Kunta Kinte", played by LeVar Burton, a lesson in manners in the opening segment of the new television mini series "Roots". (See January 23rd) 	**Silent and Sound reasons to buy a Kodak Moviedeck projector.** 	(Left) Polaroid's SX-70 Alpha Model sells for $136.88. 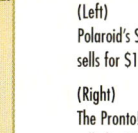 (Right) The Pronto! BC Rangefinder sells for $44.88.  Kodak Moviedeck Projector.		At the annual **College Football Bowl Games**: Rose Bowl: USC 14 - Michigan 6 Sugar Bowl: Pittsburgh 27 - Georgia 3 (Tony Dorsett sets a Sugar Bowl record running for 202 yards) Cotton Bowl: Houston 30 - Maryland 21 Orange Bowl: Ohio State 27 - Colorado 10  **1**
UPI selects the Pittsburgh Panthers, led by coach Johnny Major, as the **National Collegiate Football Champions**. The AP Poll will also select them as #1 January 3rd. USC and Michigan finish second and third in both polls. At the **Sun Bowl**, kicker Tony Franklin kicks a bowl game record-setting 62-yd field goal as Texas A&M defeats Florida 37-14. **2**	**Chart Toppers:** The #1 pop single for the eighth and final week is "Tonight's The Night" by Rod Stewart. The #1 pop album is "Songs In The Key Of Life" by Stevie Wonder for the 12th and final week. Both hits will go Platinum. NBC-TV premieres a new daytime serial **"Lovers And Friends"**. Created by Harding Lemay, the serial is set in Point Clair. **3**	A **train crash** in Chicago between two city elevated trains results in 11 deaths and 189 injuries as a train smashes into the rear of a stopped train. One car plunges 30 feet to the ground and two others are left dangling. **The 95th Congress Convenes:** Senate: 61 Democrats, 38 Republicans, 1 Independent House: 292 Democrats 143 Republicans **4**	American customers are paying an average price of $1.08 for a **5-lb bag of sugar** this year. **TV Programs Tonight On CBS:** 8:00 Good Times 8:30 Ball Four 9:00 All In The Family 9:30 Alice 10:00 The Blue Knight **5**	Frank Sinatra's mother, Natalie "Dolly" Sinatra, 82, is killed in a **plane crash** near Palm Springs, California. An AP poll selects gymnast Nadia Comanici and decathlon star Bruce Jenner as America's **female and male athletes of the year**. **6**	America's basketball clowns, the **Harlem Globetrotters**, begin their 51st season. The amazing basketball stars have become living legends capturing the hearts of the world. Their mixture of basketball skills and comedy stunts have thrilled audiences worldwide since their inception in January 1927. **7**	Kerry Reid wins the women's singles tennis title at the **Australian Open** 7-5, 6-2 over Dianne Balestrat from Australia. American Roscoe Tanner wins the men's title over top-seeded Guillermo Vilas 6-3, 6-3, 6-3. **Elvis Presley** celebrates his 42nd birthday. **8**
The **Oakland Raiders**, coached by John Madden, win their first Super Bowl 32-14 over the Minnesota Vikings in **Super Bowl XI** held in Pasadena before a record crowd of 103,438. Oakland's Fred Biletnikoff catches 4 passes for 79 yds and wins the game's MVP honors. The Vikings, coached by Bud Grant, fail in their fourth attempt to win a Super Bowl. Each Raider player receives $15,000. **9**	The Supreme Court decides 6-3 to vacate a lower Federal Appeals Court ruling that upheld the dismissal of a **homosexual** from the U.S. Civil Service. The #1 song on the Country and Western music chart is "Broken Down In Tiny Pieces" by Billy "Crash" Craddock. **10**	Utah service station operator Melvin Dummar, beneficiary of the so-called **"Mormon Will"** of billionaire Howard Hughes, admits he lied about the will, saying he delivered it to the Salt Lake City Church Headquarters where it was found April 27th, 1976. A Panamanian-registered tanker, the **"Grand Zenith"** sinks off the coast of Cape Cod, Massachussets, taking 38 lives. **11**	President Ford delivers his 3rd and final **"State of the Union"** address. Ford gives President-elect Carter his very best wishes and urges the incoming President to not let the nation's defences lag, as well as to adopt strong economic policies. Ford states "I am proud of the part I have had in rebuilding confidence in the Presidency, confidence in our free system and confidence in our future". **12**	**Chart Topper:** The #1 pop single is "You Make Me Feel Like Dancing" by Leo Sayer. An Aeroflot TU-104 airplane suddenly **explodes and crashes** over Alma-Ata in Central Asia, killing 90 passengers and crew. **13**	Claudine Longet, 35, is found guilty of criminally negligent homicide and is sentenced to 30 days in prison (at a time of her own choosing). Longet was convicted in the March 21st, 1976, shooting of former Olympic skiing champion Vladimir "Spider" Sabich, 31, who was showing Longet how to use a gun when it accidentally went off. Actor **Peter Finch** dies of a heart attack at the age of 60. **14**	Live from New York…it's **Saturday Night Live**, now in its second season with regulars John Belushi, Bill Murray, Garrett Morris, Laraine Newman, Dan Aykroyd and Jane Curtin. The "Coneheads", Connie, Beldar and Prymart, make their first appearance. Produced by Lorne Michaels on NBC, tonight's guest host is Ralph Nader with musical guest George Benson. **15**
Bruce Lietzke, 25, wins the Tucson Open golf title in a sudden-death play-off over Gene Littler. The victory is worth $40,000 in Lietzke's 1st PGA tour win. **TV Programs On CBS:** 7:00 60 Minutes 8:00 The Sonny and Cher Show 9:00 Kojak 10:00 Delvecchio **16**	After several stays of execution and two failed suicide attempts, Gary Gilmore, 36, is executed by a firing squad in Salt Lake City for the killing of Bennie Bushnell, 26, a Provo, Utah, motel clerk. Gilmore is the first American to receive capital punishment since 1967. The 17th NFL **Pro Bowl** is won by the AFC 24-17 at the Seattle Kingdome. **17**	The Centers for Disease Control in Atlanta announces the discovery of a previously unknown bacterium which is believed responsible for the **legion fever** which killed 29 during a Legionnaires Convention last July. Dr. Charles C. Shepard and Dr. Joseph E. McDade, who made the discovery, are still uncertain of the source of the microbe or its transmission. It will come to be known as "Legionnaires Disease". **18**	The first-ever-recorded **snowfall** in the city of Miami, Florida, is registered. Florida Governor Ruben Askew will estimate damages at $358 million as a result of this storm which brought in record low temperatures. **19**	**Jimmy Carter** is sworn in as the **39th President** of the United States by Chief Justice Warren E. Burger. Moments before, Walter F. Mondale was sworn in as Vice-President by House Speaker Thomas O'Neill Jr. In his inaugural address, President Carter calls for *"a new national spirit of unity and trust"*. **20**	President Carter, in his first day as President, issues a **full and unconditional pardon** to all Vietnam draft evaders who had not been involved in violent acts. Carter will receive considerable criticism from veterans groups who object to this pardon. **President Carter** is the 1st president to be elected from the deep south in 128 years. **21**	**Chart Toppers:** The #1 pop single is "I Wish" by Stevie Wonder. The #1 pop album is "Wings Over America" by Paul McCartney and Wings. The #1 R & B single is also "I Wish" by Stevie Wonder. The #1 song on the Country and Western chart is "You Never Miss A Good Thing (Till He Says Goodbye)" by Crystal Gayle. **22**
ABC-TV begins airing the new miniseries **"Roots"**. Based Alex Haley's novel, the series covers 12 hours over 8 consecutive evenings. All eight segments will be among the 15 highest-rated programs in TV history. **Tom Watson** wins the Bing Crosby Pro-Am golf event to earn $40,000. Next Sunday, he will also win the Andy Williams-San Diego Open for $36,000. **23**	Record **cold weather** has gripped most of the U.S., forcing President Carter to ask all Americans to set their thermostats at 65°F during the daytime and even lower at night in an attempt to cope with national fuel shortages. **24**	The 30th Annual NHL All-Star game is played in Vancouver, B.C. with the Wales Conference winning 4-3 over the Campbell Conference. Buffalo's Rick Martin scores two goals including the winner and is selected as the game's MVP. A new Broadway play, **"Ashes"** opens in New York City. The David Rudkin production will run for 285 performances. **25**	The hourly **minimum wage** in the United States this year is $2.30 which has been in effect since 1976. The #1 song on the Country and Western chart is "I Can't Believe She Gives It All To Me" by Conway Twitty. **26**	The **Vatican** announces that the ordination of women as Roman Catholic Priests is definitely prohibited, stating that Jesus Christ was a man and his priests had to bear a *"natural resemblance"* to him. **27**	**TV Programs Tonight On NBC:** 8:00 Sanford and Son 8:30 Chico and The Man 9:00 The Rockford Files 10:00 Serpico **Chart Toppers:** The #1 pop single is "Car Wash" by Rose Royce. **28**	Comedian **Freddie Prinze**, 22, dies of a self-inflicted gunshot wound in Los Angeles. Prinze co-starred on the popular TV show "Chico and The Man" with Jack Albertson. Roberto Duran retains his World Boxing Association (WBA) Lightweight title by knocking out Vilomar Fernandez in the 13th round during their bout in Miami. **29**
One of the **worst storms** in history continues to lash the entire U.S. By winters end, over 200" of snow will have fallen on Buffalo, New York. For the first time, satellites show snow on the ground on all 49 mainland states. The final episode of the miniseries **"Roots"** is watched by an estimated 80 million viewers to become the highest-viewed program to date in TV history. **30**	The U.S. 6th Circuit Court of Appeals in Cincinnati orders construction halted on the 90%-completed $116-million **Tellico Dam** on the Tennessee River near Knoxville. The court rules that the dam poses a threat to the "snail darter", a 3" fish (discovered in 1973 by zoologist David Etnier) which is on the Interior Dept. Endangered Species list. Construction began on the dam in 1966. **31**		Melvin Dummar admits he lied about Howard Hughes' will. (See January 11th)	1977 Volkswagen Bus		

FEBRUARY 1977

The "Enterprise" makes its maiden captive flight aboard a 747 at Edwards Air Force Base, California.

Sunday	Monday	Tuesday	Wednesday	Thursday	Friday	Saturday
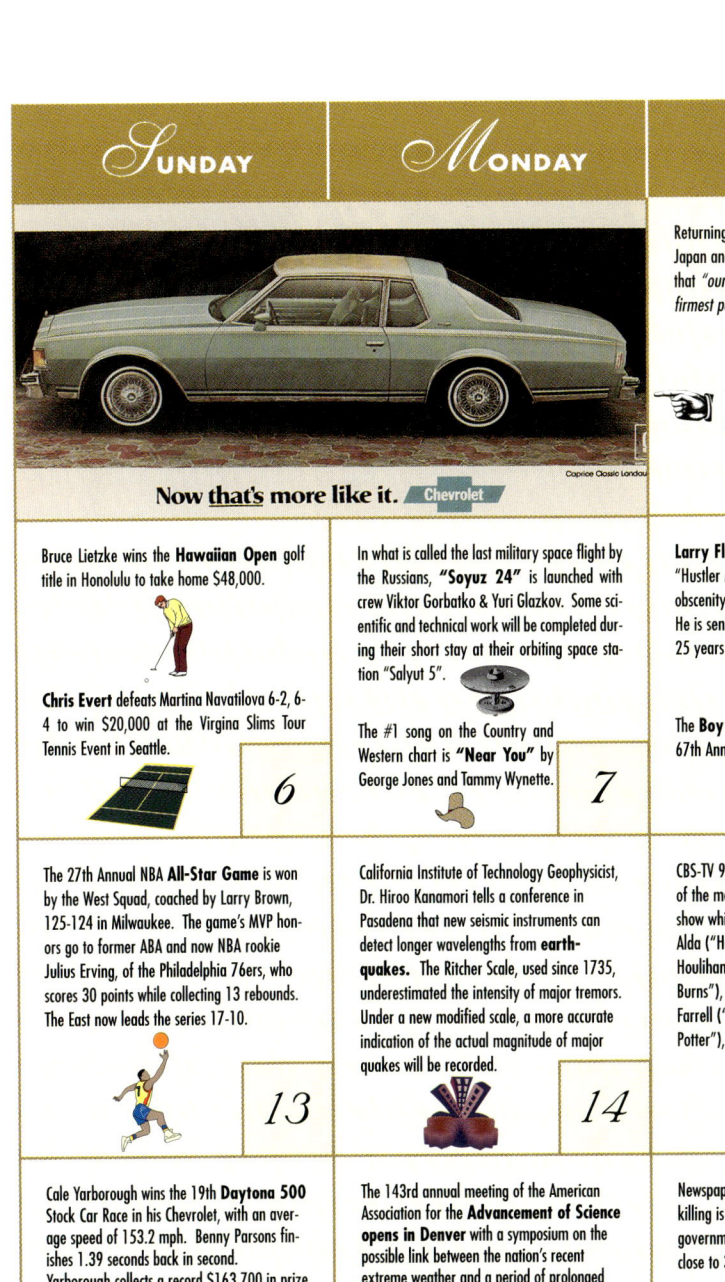 Now that's more like it. Chevrolet		Returning from a 10-day **global mission** to Japan and Europe, Vice-President Mondale says that *"our relations with our friends are on the firmest possible, most hopeful basis"*. 1977 Chevy Caprice Classic Landau Coupe **1**	Defenseman **Ian Turnbull** of the Toronto Maple Leafs sets a NHL record, becoming the first defenseman to score 5 goals in one game, as the Leafs beat the Detroit Red Wings at Toronto's Maple Leaf Gardens. A Broadway play **"Otherwise Engaged"**, written by Simon Gray, opens in New York City. The play will enjoy a run of 309 performances. BROADWAY **2**	U.S. Representative to the United Nations, **Andrew Young** from the new Carter Administration arrives in Tanzania for an 8-day visit of Africa. During his visit he will make a series of policy observations that appear to differ with administration positions. **3**	**"American Bandstand"** celebrates its Silver Anniversary with an ABC-TV special hosted by Dick Clark. Guests include Chuck Berry, Seals and Crofts, Booker T and the MG's, Johnny Rivers, The Pointer Sisters, and many more. The #1 song on the Country and Western chart is **"Let My Love Be Your Pillow"** by Ronnie Milsap. **4**	President Carter declares the city of Buffalo and its surrounding counties to be a major **disaster area**, offering aid in the cleanup of recent snowstorms. As the day goes on, the President will extend the list to include Michigan, Pennsylvania, Ohio, Indiana and southern New Jersey. **5**
Bruce Lietzke wins the **Hawaiian Open** golf title in Honolulu to take home $48,000. **Chris Evert** defeats Martina Navatilova 6-2, 6-4 to win $20,000 at the Virginia Slims Tour Tennis Event in Seattle. **6**	In what is called the last military space flight by the Russians, **"Soyuz 24"** is launched with crew Viktor Gorbatko & Yuri Glazkov. Some scientific and technical work will be completed during their short stay at their orbiting space station "Salyut 5". The #1 song on the Country and Western chart is **"Near You"** by George Jones and Tammy Wynette. **7**	**Larry Flynt**, publisher and executive editor of "Hustler Magazine", is convicted of pandering obscenity and engaging in organized crime. He is sentenced to concurrent sentences of 7 to 25 years in prison along with a $10,000 fine. The **Boy Scouts of America** celebrate their 67th Anniversary. **8**	NBC-TV premieres a new adventure program, **"The Life and Times of Grizzly Adams"**, starring Dan Haggerty as a 19th-century innocent fugitive whose best friend is a bear named "Ben". Adams has two friends "Mad Jack" (Denver Pyle) and "Nakuma" (Don Shanks), who is Adams' Indian blood brother. The program is based on the film of the same name. **9**	Chart Toppers: The #1 pop single is **"Torn Between Two Lovers"** by Mary MacGregor. The first American to set foot on the **South Pole** in 1956, Commander of the Navy's Operation Deep-Freeze Antarctic Expeditions (1955-59), Rear Adm. (Ret) George J. Dufek, 74, dies in Bethesda, Maryland. **10**	President Carter, in his first trip to Georgia as President, becomes the first to fly aboard a new **Airborne Command Post Boeing 747**, equipped with sophisticated communications equipment. A fleet of three planes, with a fourth on the way, will be made available to the Commander-In-Chief for use in a national emergency. **11**	One of the **largest lobsters** ever caught is trapped off the coast of Nova Scotia, Canada. Weighing 44 lbs, 6 oz, and measuring 3 feet 6 inches in length, it will be sold to the owner of a Bayville, New York, restaurant. **TV Programs Tonight On ABC:** 8:00 Holmes and Yoyo 8:30 Mr. T. and Tina 9:00 Starksky and Hutch 10:00 Most Wanted **12**
The 27th Annual NBA **All-Star Game** is won by the West Squad, coached by Larry Brown, 125-124 in Milwaukee. The game's MVP honors go to former ABA and now NBA rookie Julius Erving, of the Philadelphia 76ers, who scores 30 points while collecting 13 rebounds. The East now leads the series 17-10. **13**	California Institute of Technology Geophysicist, Dr. Hiroo Kanamori tells a conference in Pasadena that new seismic instruments can detect longer wavelengths from **earthquakes**. The Ritcher Scale, used since 1735, underestimated the intensity of major tremors. Under a new modified scale, a more accurate indication of the actual magnitude of major quakes will be recorded. **14**	CBS-TV 9pm: **M*A*S*H** continues to be one of the most-watched TV shows in America. The show which debuted in 1972 now stars Alan Alda ("Hawkeye"), Loretta Swit ("Maj. Houlihan"), Larry Linville ("Maj. Frank Burns"), Gary Burghoff ("Radar"), Mike Farrell ("Capt. Hunnicut") Harry Morgan ("Col. Potter"), and Jamie Farr ("Max Klinger"). **15**	A new Broadway play, **"American Buffalo"**, opens in New York City. The play will run for 135 performances. BROADWAY **TV Programs Tonight On ABC:** 8:00 The Bionic Woman 9:00 Baretta 10:00 Charlie's Angels **16**	A train carrying the "plague" approaches a bridge in **"The Cassandra Crossing"** starring Richard Harris, Sophia Loren, Burt Lancaster, Ava Gardner and Martin Sheen. Chart Toppers: The #1 pop single is **"Blinded By The Light"** by Manfred Mann's Earth Band. The #1 album is "A Star Is Born" by Barbra Streisand and Kris Kristofferson. **17**	The first U.S. test flight of the projected series of reuseable space shuttle captive flight, **"Enterprise"** makes its maiden flight attached to the top of a Boeing 747, reaching an altitude of 16,000 feet with speeds up to 280 mph. TV and film actor, widely known for his role of "Jingles" on the series "Wild Bill Hickok", **Andy Devine**, 71, dies of leukemia in Orange, California. **18**	The 19th Annual **Grammy Awards** include: Record of The Year: "This Masquerade" by George Benson Album Of The Year: "Songs In The Key Of Life" by Stevie Wonder Song Of The Year: "I Write The Songs" by Barry Manilow **19**
Cale Yarborough wins the 19th Daytona 500 Stock Car Race in his Chevrolet, with an average speed of 153.2 mph. Benny Parsons finishes 1.39 seconds back in second. Yarborough collects a record $163,700 in prize money en route to winning the Winston Cup Nascar Championship. **Tom Purtzer**, 25, wins his 1st PGA event, taking the L.A. Open golf title to win $40,000. **20**	The 143rd annual meeting of the American Association for the **Advancement of Science** opens in Denver with a symposium on the possible link between the nation's recent extreme weather and a period of prolonged inactivity on the Sun's surface. Dr. Charles Stockton, of the University of Arizona, highlights a 22-year cycle correlation with the great droughts in the dust-bowl states in the 1930's and the great drought of 1910. Jane Fonda and George Segal turn to crime in the comedy film **"Fun With Dick and Jane"**, also starring Ed McMahon, Dick Gautier, Allan Miller and John Dehner. **21**	Newspaper reports indicate that widespread killing is occurring under **Idi Amin's** Ugandan government. Sources report there have been close to 300,000 killings among various tribes. The #1 song on the Country and Western Chart is **"Moody Blue"** by Elvis Presley. **22**	Entertainer **Connie Francis** settles out of court for $1,475,000 with the Howard Johnson's Motel chain, whom Francis charged did not provide adequate security when she was raped in November 1974 at their motel in Westbury, New York. **23**	"The Marine Floridian", a 612-foot sulfur tanker, crashes into the 4,463-foot Benjamin Harrison Bridge on the James River in Hopewell, Virginia, collapsing two sections of the bridge. No one is hurt in the accident. **TV Programs Tonight On CBS:** 8:00 The Waltons 9:00 Hawaii Five-O 10:00 Barnaby Jones **24**	Ugandan President, **Idi Amin Dada**, orders all U.S. nationals in the country to meet with him in Kampala, and bars all Americans from leaving the country before then. He will lift the ban March 1st, after negotiations with U.S. representatives, and call off the meeting that was to take place at the Entebbe International Airport location. **25**	Chart Toppers: The #1 pop single is "New Kid In Town" by The Eagles. The #1 R & B single is "I've Got Love On My Mind" by Natalie Cole. The new #1 song on the Country and Western chart is **"Say You'll Stay Until Tomorrow"** by Tom Jones. **26**
The Royal Canadian Mounted Police raid the hotel room of Rolling Stone musician **Keith Richards** and seize 22 grams of heroin and 4 grams of cocaine. Richards is arrested and charged with trafficking and possession. Jack Nicklaus wins the **Jackie Gleason-Inverrary** golf title in Ft. Lauderdale earning $50,000. **27**	Eddie "Rochester" Anderson, 71, who acted as **Jack Benny's** valet during 30 years of film, radio and television broadcasting, dies of a heart ailment in Los Angeles. It is announced that the popular NBC-TV show **"The Tonight Show"**, starring Johnny Carson, will broadcast live for the first time in 18 years. **28**	Singer Barry Manilow captures "Song Of The Year" honors at the Grammy Awards for his hit "I Write The Songs". (See February 19th)			NBA rookie Julius Erving of the Philadelphia 76ers is selected as the MVP at the NBA All-Star contest in Milwaukee. (See February 13th)	

Eddie "Rochester" Anderson, seen here with Jack Benny during a 1940's film, dies in Los Angeles. (See February 28th)

MARCH 1977

Paul Newman stars as a player/coach in the new film "Slap Shot".

Sunday	Monday	Tuesday	Wednesday	Thursday	Friday	Saturday
	Actress Bette Davis receives "Life Achievement Award". (See March 1st)	**1** Sara Lowndes Dylan and her husband of 11 years, **Bob Dylan**, separate. The couple will divorce in June, giving Sara custody of their 3 children and control of their million-dollar mansion in Santa Monica, California. Actress, **Bette Davis**, 68, is presented with a "Life Achievement Award" by the American Film Institute, becoming the first woman to receive the honor.	**2** Hank Williams Sr. is awarded a **Gold Record** for his hit album "24 Greatest Hits". Officials in West Berlin announce that $575,000 has been raised to help American victims suffering through severe winter weather.	**3** **Coffee prices** in the U.S. are at a record high price of $3.71 per pound. On January 20th the price was $3.11 per pound. The cost of imported green coffee beans had increased due to a current worldwide shortage. A Kuwait tanker "Borag" has spilled over **10,000 tons** of oil offshore near Taiwan after breaking up when it hit a reef.	**4** Chart Toppers: The #1 pop single is "Love Theme from A Star Is Born (Evergreen)" by Barbra Streisand. Many Americans are participating in a "**Turn the TV off**" week that was initiated by Mississippi Rev. Donald Wildman. The boycott is aimed at the "deterioration of programming".	**5** A 2-hour call-in radio show between President Carter and 42 citizens is broadcast from the White House. CBS anchorman Walter Cronkite is the moderator of the experimental program called "**Ask President Carter**", with questions ranging from politics to personal topics. AT&T report that close to 9.5 million attempts were made by Americans to dial into the show.
6 "New York Times" Best-Sellers List: Paperback 1) "The Final Days" by Bob Woodward and Carl Bernstein 2) "Moonstruck Madness" by Laurie McBain Fiction 1) "Trinity" by Leon Uris 2) "Raise The Titanic" by Clive Cussler General 1) "Roots" by Alex Haley 2) "Passages" by Gail Sheehy	**7** President Carter meets with Israeli Premier Yitzhak Rabin in Washington to discuss the possibility of reconvening the Geneva **Peace Conference** on Middle East. A California Agriculture Department spokesman predicts that **drought-related losses** could reach $6 billion in agriculture alone.	**8** The 5 top-rated **television shows** in the U.S. at this time are: 1) Happy Days 2) Laverne and Shirley 3) ABC Monday Night At The Movies 4) M*A*S*H 5) Charlie's Angels The #1 song on the Country and Western chart is "**Heart Healer**" by Mel Tillis.	**9** The U.S. Food and Drug Administration (FDA) proposes a ban on the use of the artificial sweetener **saccharin** as Canadian tests show that rats fed high dosages of the sweetener developed cancerous bladder tumors. Americans currently consume five million pounds of saccharin each year.	**10** Cornell University astronomers discover through observations made from a 36" telescope, carried by a C-141 aircraft to 41,000 feet to avoid most atmospheric distortion, that the **planet Uranus** has rings thought to circle the planet at a distance of 11,000 to 16,000 miles above the planet's cloud cover. NASA says the rings are "the first major structures in the solar system to be found since the discovery of the planet Pluto in 1930".	**11** Rose Elizabeth Bird, 40, is confirmed as the **first woman** Chief Justice of the California Supreme Court. Susie Sharp, Chief Justice of North Carolina, is the only other female currently holding such a judicial position. The Centers for Disease Control in Atlanta report that there has been a serious outbreak of **Reye's syndrome** this year. 152 cases in 33 states have been cited, including 18 deaths.	**12** With 100 mph winds and 25-foot snowdrifts, the **most severe snowstorm** of the winter hits the midwestern states of Colorado, Nebraska, Kansas and South Dakota. George C. Scott stars in the film version of Hemingway's novel "**Islands In The Stream**", co-starring David Hemmings, Claire Bloom, Susan Tyrrell, Gilbert Roland and Richard Evans.
13 Andy Bean wins his first PGA golf event, the **Doral Open**, in Miami on his 24th birthday. Bean picks up $40,000 for his victory. The U.S. sweeps the **Aetna World Cup Tennis Challenge** against Australia in 7 straight matches. The title was clinched when Jimmy Conners defeated Tony Roche yesterday.	**14** The Carter Administration calls for the decriminalization of **marijuana** use, believing that the possession of an ounce or less should be subject to fines, rather than jail sentences. The Administration is also going to re-evaluate its position on cocaine use, since it is also thought to be a non-addictive drug.	**15** ABC-TV premieres a new sitcom entitled "Three's Company" about a young man living in L.A. who shares an apartment with two girls. The series stars John Ritter as "Jack Tripper" with Joyce DeWitt as "Janet" and Suzanne Somers as "Chrissy". Based on a British comedy "Man About The House", their landlord "Stanley Roper" played by Norman Fell allows the living arrangements because he believes "Jack" is gay.	**16** Chart Toppers: The #1 pop single continues to be "Evergreen" by Barbra Streisand. The #1 pop album is "A Star Is Born" by Kris Kristofferson and Barbra Streisand. The #1 R & B single is "I've Got Love On My Mind" by Natalie Cole. The #1 song on the Country and Western chart is "**She's Just An Old love Turned Memory**" by Charley Pride.	**17** Former World Heavyweight Champion, **George Foreman** is defeated by Jimmy Young in their 12-round bout in San Juan, Puerto Rico. The bullet-riddled body of **Al Bramlet's**, President of the Nevada State AFL-CIO who disappeared February 24th, is found in the Nevada desert.	**18** President Carter **removes the ban** on U.S. citizens from travelling to Cuba, Vietnam, North Korea and Cambodia, in support of the 1975 Helsinki Accords that called for improved human rights.	**19** Paul Newman is the coach and star of a bush-league hockey team stuck in last place until they decide to play dirty in "**Slap Shot**" with Michael Ontkean, Lindsay Crouse, Jennifer Warren, Melinda Dillon, Strother Martin and Jerry Houser. The movie is directed by George Roy Hill.
20 St. Bonaventure University wins the 40th Annual NIT Basketball title defeating the University of Houston 94-91 at Madison Square Garden in New York City. St. Boneventure is led by forward Greg Sanders, who scores 40 pts. and grabs 12 rebounds to win the MVP honors. Mark Haye wins the **Players Championship** in Jacksonville, Florida.	**21** **President Carter** meets with Japanese Premier Takeo Fukud in Washington to discuss the U.S. military presence in the western Pacific, as well as atomic energy and Japanese export practices. TV Programs Tonight On NBC: 8:00 Little House On The Prairie 9:00 NBC Monday Night Movie	**22** India's Prime Minister **Indira Gandhi** resigns her position after her Congress Party was defeated by the opposition Janata Party in national elections. Head of the party, Morarji R. Desai will be selected as India's new Prime Minister on March 24th. The Supreme Court of Canada rules against allowing evidence obtained by lie detector tests to be used in murder trials.	**23** The ABC-TV crime show "**Charlie's Angels**" continues to be one of the nation's most-watched programs. Kate Jackson ("Sabrina"), Farrah Fawcett ("Jill") and Jaclyn Smith ("Kelly") star as 3 detectives who take cases from associate David Doyle ("Bosley") who receives them from their "unseen boss" voiced by John Forsythe. **Short water supplies** in the Texas panhandle high plains region threaten farms that produce 20% of the country's cotton and sorghum.	**24** Film director **Roman Polanski**, 43, widower of murdered Sharon Tate, is indicted on rape, sodomy and other felony charges in connection with an alleged attack of a 13-year-old girl he was photographing for a French magazine.	**25** Film producer and screenwriter who wrote film scripts including "The Grapes of Wrath", "Tobacco Road" and "The Dirty Dozen", **Nunnally Johnson**, 79, dies of pneumonia in Los Angeles. Johnson also wrote, directed, and produced "The Three Faces of Eve".	**26** Chart Toppers: The #1 pop single is "Rich Girl" by Hall and Oates. The #1 pop album is "Hotel California" by The Eagles. The #1 R & B single is "I've Got Love On My Mind" by Natalie Cole. The #1 song on the Country and Western chart is "**Southern Nights**" by Glen Campbell.
27 The world's worst **aviation disaster** in history occurs as a KLM Royal Dutch Airlines Boeing 747 slams into a Pan Am Boeing 747, flying in dense fog as it taxies on the runway at the Los Rodeos Airport on the Canary Island of Tenerife, killing 579 people. All 248 passengers and crew aboard the landing KLM plane are killed. 70 people survive on the Pan-Am plane that carried mostly Americans on a charter from L.A.	**28** The 49th Academy Award Oscars include: Best Picture: "Rocky" United Artists Director: John C. Avildsen "Rocky" Actress: Faye Dunaway "Network" Actor: Peter Finch "Network" The 39th NCAA **Basketball Championship** is won by the Marquette Warriors 67-59 over the North Carolina Tar Heels at Atlanta's Omni Arena.	**29** A private research organization releases information indicating that women over the age of 30 who are taking birth control pills and smoking cigarettes face a significantly **higher death rate**. TV Programs Tonight On NBC: 8:00 Baa Baa, Black Sheep 9:00 Police Woman 10:00 Police Story	**30** At the Annual NFL Team Owners **Spring Meeting** in Phoenix, the sale of the San Francisco 49ers to Edward Debartolo Jr. is approved. Tampa Bay is moved from the AFC West to the NFC Central and the Seattle Seahawks from the NFC West to the AFC West Division. The season is expanded from 14 games to 16 games.	**31** **Karen Anne Quinlan**, who went into a coma on April 14th, 1975, and whose parents won a long court battle to have the mechanical respirator turned off March 31st, 1976, is still alive one year later, weighing just 70 lbs. Quinlan's parents believed that the machine was preventing their daughter from dying with "decency and dignity".		

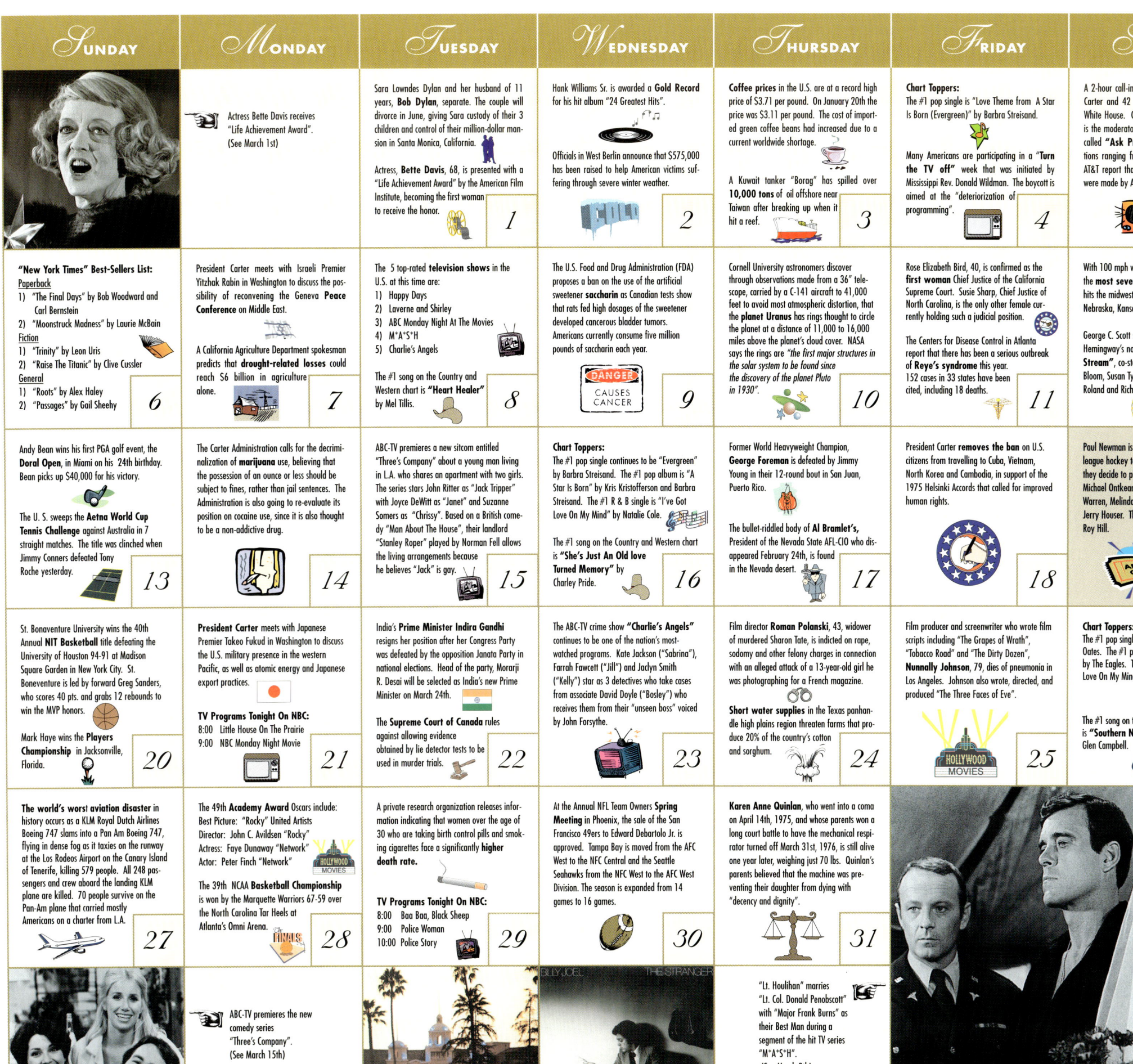

ABC-TV premieres the new comedy series "Three's Company". (See March 15th)

The LP "Hotel California" by The Eagles tops the Album Music Chart. (See March 26th)

"Lt. Houlihan" marries "Lt. Col. Donald Penobscott" with "Major Frank Burns" as their Best Man during a segment of the hit TV series "M*A*S*H". (See March 8th)

The LP "The Stranger" by Billy Joel.

APRIL 1977

Diane Keaton and Woody Allen star in the new film "Annie Hall".

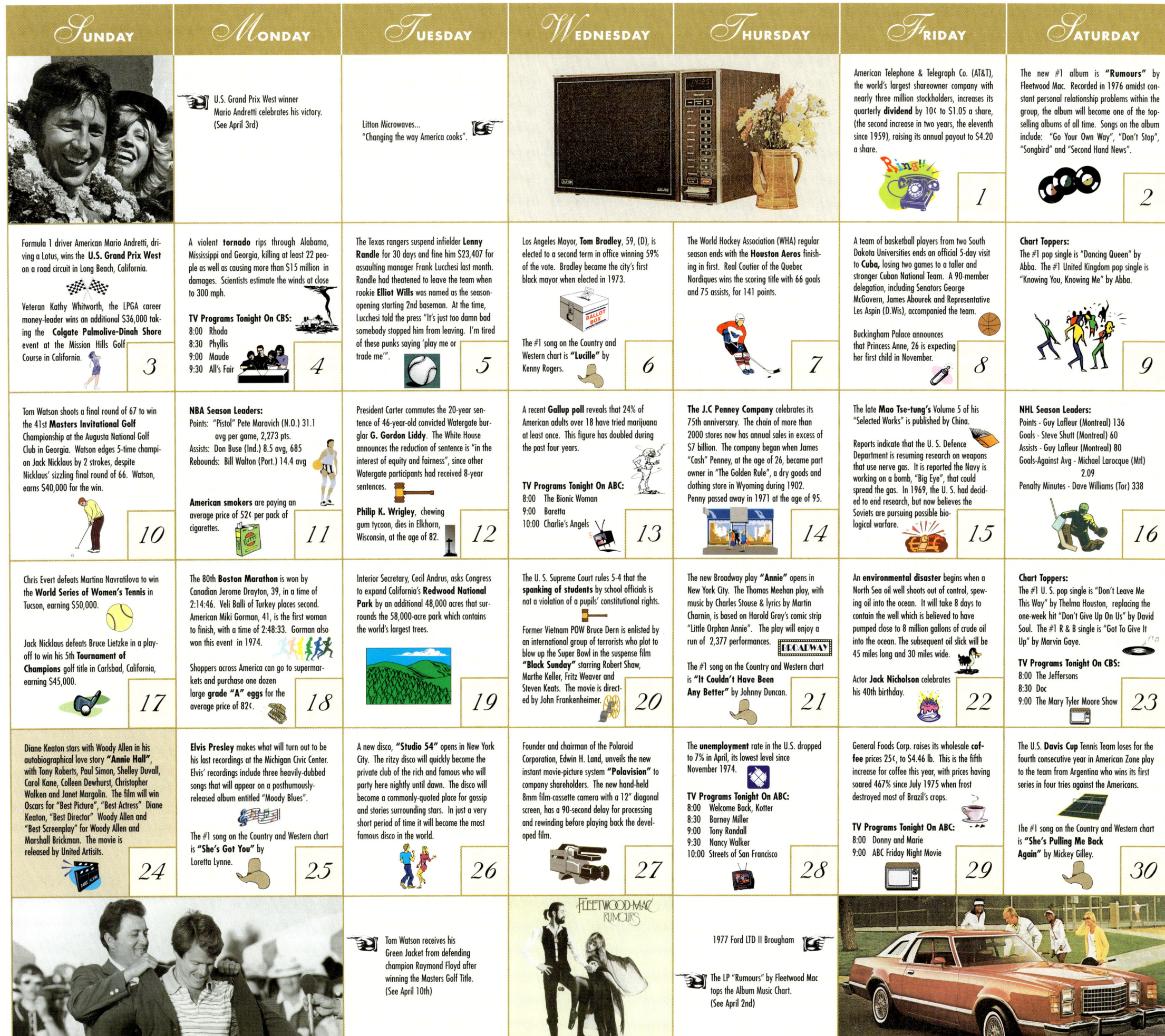

MAY 1977

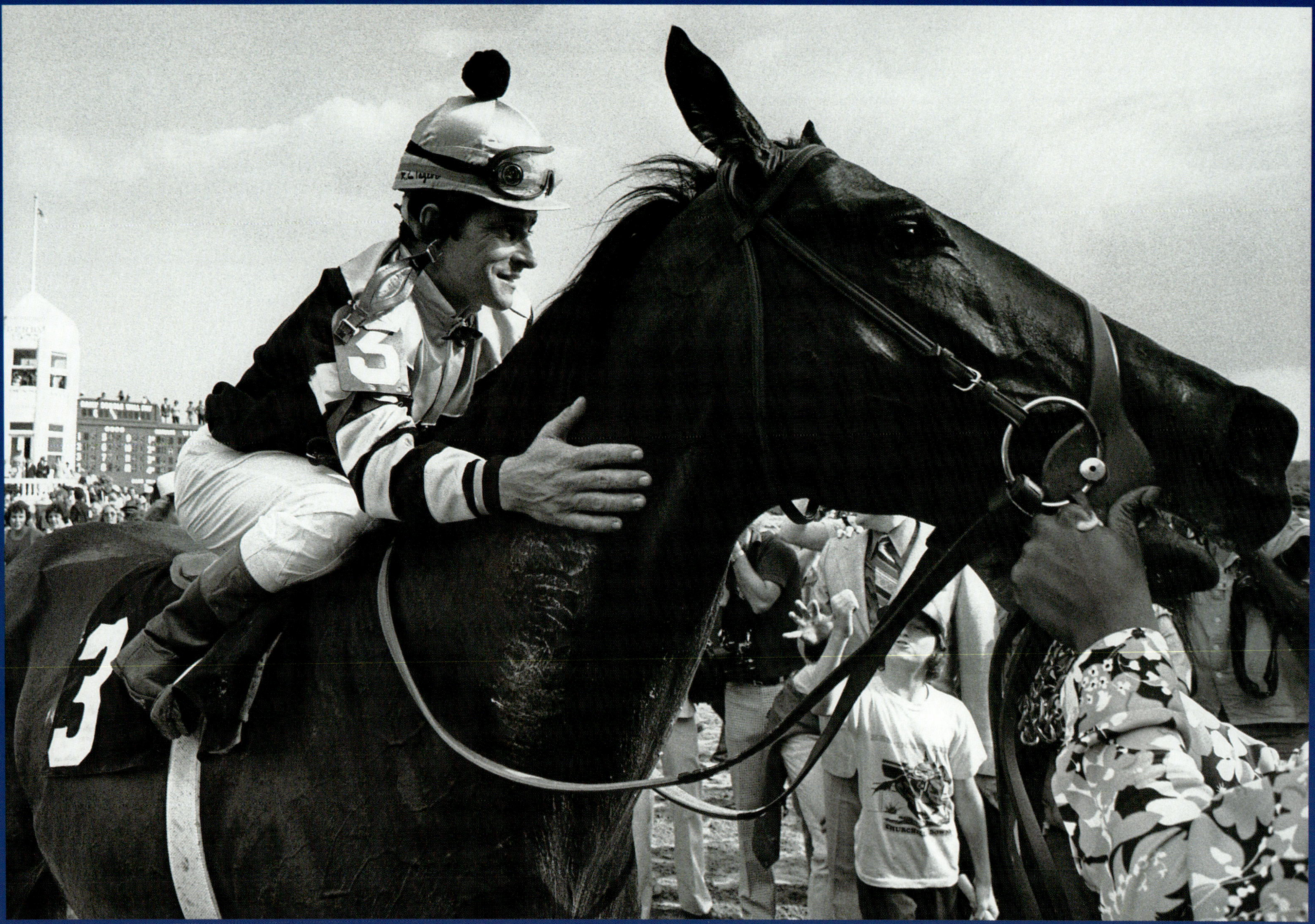

"Seattle Slew" with jockey Jean Cruguet aboard captures the "Kentucky Derby" enroute to the Triple Crown.

Sunday	Monday	Tuesday	Wednesday	Thursday	Friday	Saturday
The **Dalai Lama**, in exile in India following a 1959 revolt, is invited by China to return to Tibet, if he will accept Chinese Communist authority in the Autonomous Region. Gene Littler wins the **Houston Open** golf title. Jimmy Conners defeats Raul Ramirez to win $50,000 at the **Alan King-Caesar's Palace** tennis event. **1**	Culminating two days of protests, 1,414 members of a group known as the **Clamshell Alliance** are arrested by authorities at the construction site of the nuclear power plant in Seabrook, New Hampshire. The group is arrested as part of the nation's first massive show of civil disobedience against nuclear plant construction. **2**	At the annual **NFL draft** of college players in New York City, the Tampa Bay Buccaneers (0-14 last season) select running-back Rickey Bell from USC. Seattle trades the #2 pick overall to the Dallas Cowboys who select Heisman Trophy-winner record-setting running-back Tony Dorsett from Pittsburgh University. The 1st quarterback selected is Steve Pisarkiewicz by St. Louis with the 19th pick. **3**	Many Americans watch a nationally-televised interview between former U.S. President **Richard M. Nixon** and British television celebrity **David Frost**. Frost repeatedly challenges Nixon with quotes from the Presidential tape recordings. Nixon admits he had *"let the American people down"*, but he did not commit any criminal or impeachable offense. **4**	California suffers its worst **drought** on record as river and stream flows are measured at 87% below normal. Northern California has received 19 inches of rain during the year compared with a normal rainfall of 57.6 inches. Ace Hollywood stuntman Hal Needham makes his directorial debut in the action-packed film **"Smokey and The Bandit"**, starring Burt Reynolds, Sally Field, Jackie Gleason and Paul Williams. **5**	The FDA will continue to ban the sale of **Laetrile** in the U.S. Many people believe that Laetrile, which is also known as B-17 can prevent or cure cancer, but government studies have found the treatment to be virtually worthless. Available in 26 countries, many Americans are smuggling Laetrile in from Mexico. The U.S. sues the city of Detroit over **sewage leakages** into Lake Erie and the Detroit River. **6**	**"Seattle Slew"** with jockey Jean Cruguet aboard wins the 103rd **Kentucky Derby**, running the 1 1/4-mile distance in a time of 2:02 1/5. "Run Dusty Run" places second with "Sanhedrin" finishing third. The Montreal Canadiens, led by Yvon Lambert's 2 goals, defeat the visiting Boston Bruins 7-3 in game one of the NHL **Stanley Cup** finals. **7**
Raymond Floyd wins the **Byron Nelson Golf Classic** in Dallas, taking home the $40,000 1st prize. **TV Programs Tonight On NBC:** 7:00 The Wonderful World of Disney 8:00 NBC Sunday Night Movie (McCloud) 9:30 The Big Event **8**	**Chart Toppers:** The #1 pop single is "Hotel California" by The Eagles who also have a top album by the same name. The #1 R & B single is "Got To Give It Up" by Marvin Gaye. The #1 song on the Country and Western chart is **"Play, Guitar, Play"** by Conway Twitty. **9**	**The Canadiens** at home in the Montreal Forum shut out the Bruins 3-0, with Steve Shutt scoring 1 goal and adding 2 assists. Goalie Ken Dryden records the shutout. Actress **Joan Crawford**, 73, dies in New York City. During her illustrious career, Crawford appeared in more than 80 films, including her Oscar-winning performance as "Mildred Pierce" in 1945. **10**	The best-of-seven series for the World Hockey Association (WHA) championship gets under way in Quebec City between the defending champion **Winnipeg Jets** and the Quebec Nordiques. The Jets win 2-1 but will go on to lose in the seventh and deciding game on May 24th to the Nordiques who win the Avco Cup, led by Serge Bernier who wins the MVP honors. **11**	The visiting **Montreal Canadiens**, coached by Scotty Bowman, take a commanding 3-0 Stanley Cup series lead with a 4-2 win over the Boston Bruins, who are coached by Don Cherry. Guy Lafleur scores 2 goals and adds 2 assists against Boston goalie Gerry Cheevers. **12**	**"Hustler Magazine"** publisher Larry Flynt sends letters to 10 beautiful women, including rock singer Linda Ronstadt, offering each of them $1 million to be photographed in the nude for his magazine. Ronstadt will respond by tossing his offer into the garbage. **13**	**Chart Toppers:** The #1 pop single is "When I Need You" by Leo Sayer. Jacques Lemaire scores his second goal of the game at 4:32 of overtime, to give the visiting **Montreal Canadiens** a 2-0 win over the Boston Bruins and their second straight Stanley Cup. Conn Smythe Trophy-winner Guy Lafleur leads all play-off scorers with 26 points. **14**
NBC has cancelled the scheduled telecast tonight of the TV **Emmy** Awards due to a conflict between NBC and elements of the 12,000-member academy who had decided to boycott voting on the Emmy's and to stay away from the award ceremony. Ben Crenshaw rallies from a late round collapse at last week's **Byron Nelson**, to win the **Colonial Invitational** at Ft. Worth, Texas. **15**	Two-time World Heavyweight Boxing Champ, **Muhammad Ali**, 35, (221 1/4 lbs), wins a 15-round unanimous decision over Alfredo Evangelista, (209 1/4 lbs), in Landover, Maryland. A New York Airways **helicopter** idling atop the 59-story Pan-Am Building tips over, breaking a 20-foot rotor blade which slashes 4 people to death on the landing pad. **16**	Israel's Right Wing Likud Party, led by **Menachem Begin**, 63, wins a close national election in Israel. The ruling Labour Party had been in power since the state of Israel was formed during 1948. **TV Programs Tonight On ABC:** 8:00 Happy Days 8:30 Laverne and Shirley 9:00 Rich Man, Poor Man 10:00 Family **17**	The NBA **Rookie Of The Year** award for the regular season goes to Buffalo's Adrian Dantley, whose Braves finished the year with a dismal 30-52 mark. New Orleans had selected Dantley as their #1 pick in the 1976 draft out of Notre Dame. The #1 song on the Country and Western chart is **"Some Broken Hearts Never Mend"** by Don Williams. **18**	Sandra Ilene West, 37, a **millionairess** who died March 10th, is buried in San Antonio, Texas, dressed in a lace nightgown and seated in her 1964 Ferrari sports car. The unusual request is conducted according to her wishes, set out in a $2.6-million will. **19**	A sabotaged private luxury jet sinks to the bottom of the ocean in the 3rd made-to-order disaster epic, **"Airport 77"**, starring Jack Lemmon, Lee Grant, Brenda Vaccaro, George Kennedy, James Stewart, Joseph Cotten, Olivia de Havilland and Darren McGavin. The movie is directed by Jerry Jameson. **20**	A record crowd of 77,346 turns out to see "**Seattle Slew**", with Jean Cruguet aboard, win the 102nd **Preakness Stakes** Horse Race for 3-year-olds, running the 1 3/16-mile distance in a time of 1:54 2/5 to take home the $138,600 first prize. Second place goes to "Iron Constitution" with "Run Dusty Run" placing third in the historic stakes race first run in 1873. **21**
The Philadelphia 76ers edge the visiting Portland Trail Blazers 107-101 in game one of the **NBA** finals. Jack Nicklaus captures the **Memorial Golf Championship** in Dubin, Ohio, becoming golf's first $3-million career-winner. Harvard wins the 112th Harvard-Yale **Rowing Race** in New London, Connecticut. **22**	The NBA **Podoloff Cup**, awarded to the league's "most valuable player" as selected by the players themselves, goes once again to Kareem Abdul Jabbar. The veteran L.A. Laker wins his fifth honor, equalling the great Boston Celtic legend Bill Russell. Gordie Howe, 49, signs a new contract with the New England Whalers to play with sons Marty, 23 and Mark 22. **23**	**The NHL All-Star Team:** Goal - Ken Dryden (Montreal) Defense - Larry Robinson (Montreal) Borje Salming (Toronto) Center - Marcel Dionne (L.A.) Right Wing - Guy Lafleur (Montreal) Left Wing - Steve Shutt (Montreal) **24**	The fourth and last in the weekly series of nationally-televised conversations between David Frost and former President **Richard Nixon** takes place. A fifth taped interview will be aired on September 3rd. Captain of the West German team that won the 1974 World Cup of Soccer, **Franz Beckenbauer** signs a contract with the Cosmos of the North American Soccer League. **25**	The home-court **Philadelphia 76ers** blast the Portland Trail Blazers 107-89 to take a 2-0 lead in the best-of-seven NBA World Championship series. A brawl breaks out between Darryl Dawkins and Maurice Lucas that spreads to involve several players and fans. **26**	Canadian Prime Minister Pierre Trudeau and his wife Margaret legally separate ending six years of marriage. President Carter takes a 9-hour ride aboard the nuclear submarine **"U.S.S. Los Angeles"**. **27**	Fire breaks out at the **Beverly Hills Supper Club** in Southgate, Kentucky, killing 161 people, mostly from smoke inhalation. This is the worst nightclub fire since 1942 when 491 died at the Coconut Grove in Boston. Sue Press incredibly scores **2 back-to-back holes-in-one** on the 13th and 14th holes of the Chatswood Golf Course in Sydney, Australia. **28**
The 61st **Indianapolis 500** is won for a record 4th time (1961, 1964, 1967) by A.J. Foyt. For the first time at Indy, a woman races as Janet Guthrie, 39, lasts 27 laps before she has mechanical problems. Portland pounds the visiting 76ers 129-107 in game 3 of the **NBA** finals. Elvis Presley walks off the stage in Baltimore. **29**	Right-hander Dennis Eckersley of the Cleveland Indians tosses a superb 2-0 **no-hitter** over the visiting California Angels. The #1 song on the Country and Western chart is **"Luckenbach Texas (Back to the Basics of Love)"** by Waylon Jennings. **30**	The home-court **Portland Trail Blazers** destroy the Philadelphia 76ers 130-98, to even their NBA championship series at two games apiece. Second-year star Bill Walton continues to spearhead the attack for Portland. **31**				

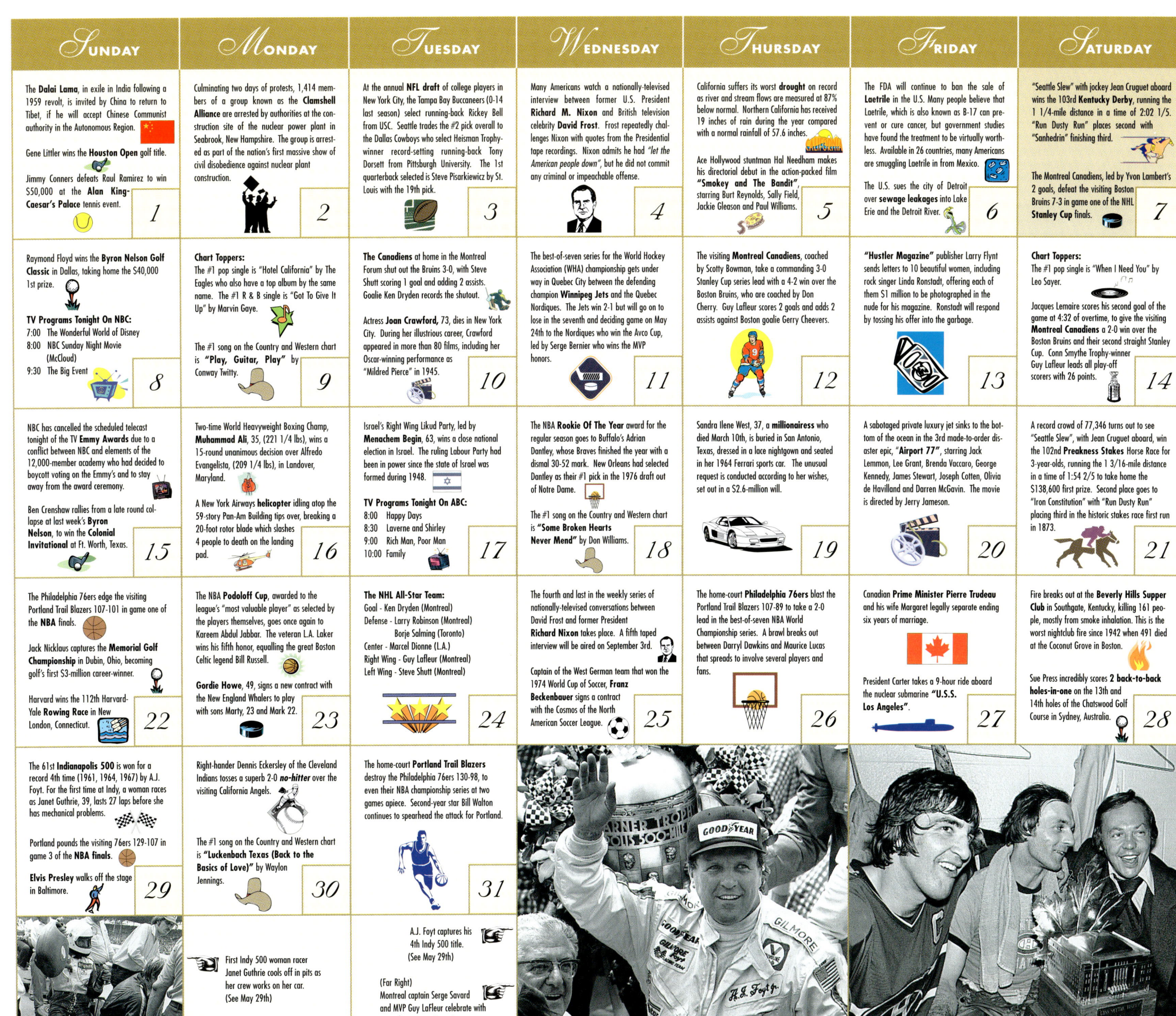

First Indy 500 woman racer Janet Guthrie cools off in pits as her crew works on her car. (See May 29th)

A.J. Foyt captures his 4th Indy 500 title. (See May 29th)

(Far Right) Montreal captain Serge Savard and MVP Guy LaFleur celebrate with injured teammate Yvan Cournoyer following their Stanley Cup victory. (See May 14th)

JUNE 1977

Mark Hamill, Carrie Fisher and Harrison Ford star in the new space adventure film "Star Wars".

Sunday	Monday	Tuesday	Wednesday	Thursday	Friday	Saturday
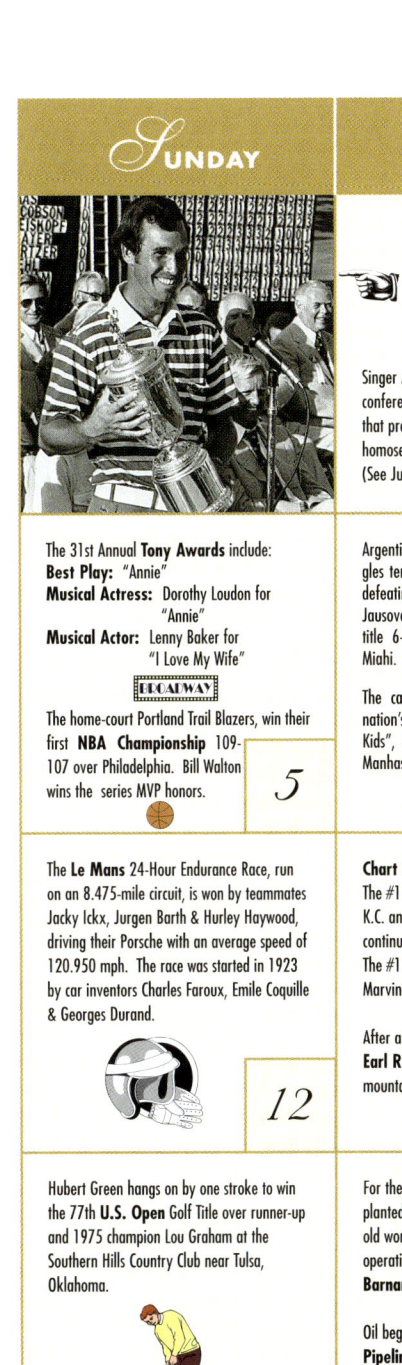	Hubert Green celebrates his U.S. Open Golf title victory. (See June 19th) Singer **Anita Bryant** appears at a press conference after repeal of an ordinance that prohibited discrimination against homosexuals. (See June 7th)		The National Institute on Alcohol Abuse and Alcoholism warns that pregnant women who have two or more drinks a day during pregnancy risk giving birth to deformed or retarded children. Authorities call the risk and consequent abnormalities *"Fetal Alcohol Syndrome"* which increases with the amount of alcohol consumed. **1**	**Chart Toppers:** The #1 pop single for the 3rd consecutive week is "Sir Duke" by Stevie Wonder. The #1 pop album is "Rumours" by Fleetwood Mac. The #1 R & B single is also "Sir Duke" by Stevie Wonder. **American Motors Corporation** announces that it intends to lay off 3,000 workers for 1 week. In April, 4,000 were laid off due to "sluggish car sales". **2**	The visiting Portland Trail Blazers win their third straight game in the championship series, defeating Philadelphia 110-104. Portland now leads the **NBA Finals** series 3-2. A recent Agriculture Department report indicates **U.S. coffee consumption** has fallen 17% during the 1st three months of this year. Sharp price increases are cited as the reason for the decline. **3**	The **best-selling** mass market paperback books in the U.S. at this time are: 1) "The Deep" by Peter Benchley 2) "The Warriors" by John Jakes 3) "The Hite Report" by Shere Hite 4) "The Lonely Lady" by Harold Robbins 5) "Dolores" by Jacqueline Susann **4**
The 31st Annual Tony Awards include: Best Play: "Annie" Musical Actress: Dorothy Loudon for "Annie" Musical Actor: Lenny Baker for "I Love My Wife" The home-court Portland Trail Blazers, win their first **NBA Championship** 109-107 over Philadelphia. Bill Walton wins the series MVP honors. **5**	Argentina's Guillermo Vilas wins the men's singles tennis title at the **French Open** in Paris, defeating Brian Gottfried 6-0, 6-3, 6-0. Mima Jausovec of Yugoslavia captures the women's title 6-2, 6-7, 6-1 over Romania's Forenza Miahi. The cartoonist who for 25 years drew the nation's oldest comic strip, "The Katzenjammer Kids", **Joe Musial**, 72, dies in Manhasset, New York. **6**	The citizens of Dade County, Florida, vote by a margin of 2-1 to repeal an ordinance that prohibited discrimination against homosexuals. Prior to this vote, singer **Anita Bryant** had raised a significant public outcry against the ordinance which had received national attention. Following the overturning of the law, Bryant says *"with God's help we will prevail in our fight to repeal similar laws throughout the nation".* **7**	Mark Hamill stars as Luke Skywalker in the film **"Star Wars"**, produced and directed by George Lucas, with Harrison Ford, Carrie Fisher, Peter Cushing, Alex Guinness, Anthony Daniels, Kenny Baker and the voice of James Earl Jones as "Darth Vader". The film will win seven Oscars, mostly for technical achievement along with "Best Score" for John Williams. The movie is released by 20th Century-Fox. **8**	NHL Trophy Winners For This Season: Hart Memorial (MVP) - Guy Lafleur (Montreal) Art Ross (Scoring) - Guy Lafleur (Montreal) Vezina (Goalie) - Ken Dryden (Montreal) Michel "Bunny" LaRocque (Mtl) James Norris (Defense) - Larry Robinson (Mtl) Calder Memorial (Rookie) - Willi Plett (Atlanta) Lady Byng (Sportsmanship) - Marcel Dionne (L.A.) **9**	**James Earl Ray**, convicted killer of Martin Luther King Jr., serving a 99-year sentence, escapes from the Brushy Mountain State Prison. First Lady **Rosalynn Carter** continues on her 7-country Latin American tour, visiting Colombia to discuss the 70 Americans who are imprisoned there on "drug smuggling" charges. **10**	"Seattle Slew" with jockey Jean Cruguet aboard wins the 109th Belmont Stakes, running the 1 1/2-mile track in 2:29 3/5. "Run Dusty Run" places second with "Sanhedrin" finishing third. "Seattle Slew" becomes the 10th horse, and first since "Secretariat" in 1973, to win horse racing's Triple Crown. "Seattle Slew" is the offspring of "Bold Reasoning" and "My Charmer". **11**
The Le Mans 24-Hour Endurance Race, run on an 8.475-mile circuit, is won by teammates Jacky Ickx, Jurgen Barth & Hurley Haywood, driving their Porsche with an average speed of 120.950 mph. The race was started in 1923 by car inventors Charles Faroux, Emile Coquille & Georges Durand. **12**	**Chart Toppers:** The #1 pop single is "I'm Your Boogie Man" by K.C. and The Sunshine Band. The #1 album continues to be "Rumours" by Fleetwood Mac. The #1 R & B single is "Got To Give It Up" by Marvin Gaye. After an intense manhunt, fugitive **James Earl Ray** is recaptured in the mountains. **13**	**Alan Reed**, the voice of the popular television cartoon character "Fred Flintstone", dies. ABC-TV 8:30pm: **"Laverne and Shirley"** continues to be one of the most-watched TV shows. Premiering in 1976, the series stars Penny Marshall ("Laverne") and Cindy Williams ("Shirley") as two 1950's girls working in a Milwaukee brewery. Other stars include David Landers ("Squiggy") and Michael McKean ("Lenny"). **14**	Motorcar enthusiasts are paying an average of 66¢ per gallon of regular unleaded **gasoline** this year to fuel their automobiles. The average mileage per gallon of gas is 14 miles for passenger cars. Country and Western entertainer Waylon Jennings celebrates his 40th birthday. **15**	The U.S.S.R. announces that Communist General Secretary, **Leonid Brezhnev**, 70, has been elected President of the Soviet Union by both houses of the Supreme Soviet, replacing Nikolai Podgorny. German-born pioneer in rocketry, designer of the U2 missiles fired on London in 1944, **Wernher Von Braun** dies in Alexandria, Virginia. **16**	The Top 5 Songs On The Pop Music Chart Are: 1) "Dreams" - Fleetwood Mac 2) "Got To Give It Up" - Marvin Gaye 3) "Gonna Fly Now" (Theme From The Film "Rocky") - by Bill Conti 4) "Feels Like The First Time" - by Foreigner 5) "Lucille" - by Kenny Rogers **17**	During a game in Boston, NY Yankee manager **Billy Martin** and team slugger **Reggie Jackson** are involved in a dugout "altercation". **A forest fire** that destroys 12,000 acres of New Mexico's timberland comes to within 800 yards of an explosives storage unit at the government's nuclear research facility known as Los Alamos Scientific Laboratory. **18**
Hubert Green hangs on by one stroke to win the 77th **U.S. Open** Golf Title over runner-up and 1975 champion Lou Graham at the Southern Hills Country Club near Tulsa, Oklahoma. **19**	For the first time, a baboon's heart is transplanted into the body of a human. A 26-year-old woman dies 2 1/2 hours after the 12-hour operation performed by **Dr. Christiaan Barnard.** Oil begins flowing through the **Trans-Alaska Pipeline** from the Prudhoe Bay Field on Alaska's north slope to the Port of Valdez, 789 miles away. **20**	The film adaptation of Peter Benchley's novel **"The Deep"** stars Jacqueline Bisset and Nick Nolte. The film, directed by Peter Yates also stars Robert Shaw, Louis Gossett, Eli Wallach, and Robert Tessier. The movie is released by Columbia. The demon still lives inside Linda Blair in the film sequel to the 1973 hit, **"Exorcist II: The Heretic"** co-starring Richard Burton. **21**	Steven Petrosino drinks one liter of beer in 1.3 seconds at The Gingerbreadman in Carlisle, Pennsylvania. **John A. Ziegler Jr.**, 43, is elected President of the NHL succeeding Clarence S. Campbell, 72, who had been President since 1945. Ziegler, the league's Chairman of the Board since 1976, is the first "American" President. **22**	Former U.S. Attorney General, **John N. Mitchell**, 63, enters the minimum security prison at Maxwell Air Force Base near Montgomery, Alabama, to serve his sentence for his role in the Watergate cover-up. H.R. Haldeman, former White House Chief of Staff, began his 30-month-to-8-year sentence yesterday at the minimum security prison at Lompoc, California. **23**	The NBA First All-Star Team: Kareem Abdul Jabbar - Los Angeles Pete Maravich - New Orleans Paul Westphal - Phoenix Elvin Hayes - Washington David Thompson - Denver **24**	Pro basketball player **Ted St. Martin** of Jacksonville, Florida, shoots 2,036 consecutive free throws during a demonstration. A large cast including Dirk Bogarde, James Caan, Michael Caine, Sean Connery, Elliot Gould, Gene Hackman, and Robert Redford star in the British war film **"A Bridge Too Far"**. The movie is directed by Richard Attenborough. **25**
Elvis Presley makes what will be his last public appearance when he performs at the Market Square Arena in Indianapolis. Tom Watson wins the **Western Open** golf title in Oakbrook, Illinois, to take the $40,000 1st prize. **26**	**The U.S. Supreme Court** votes 5-4 that lawyers cannot be constitutionally prevented from advertising their fees for routine legal services. In April, Chief Justice Warren Burger instructed the group that unless more legal disputes are settled outside the courtroom, the country could be *"overrun by hordes of lawyers as hungry as locusts"*. **27**	New York City police hunt for a psychopathic killer who calls himself **"Son of Sam"**. The self-proclaimed killer has taken five lives and wounded six others with a .44 caliber revolver since July 1976. **28**	**Chart Toppers:** The #1 pop single is "Got To Give It Up" by Marvin Gaye. The #1 pop album is "Rumours" by Fleetwood Mac. The #1 R & B single is "Best Of My Love" by The Emotions. The **Supreme Court** rules 7-2 that a man cannot be sentenced to death for the rape of an adult woman. **29**	A consumer group launches a $1-billion lawsuit against the makers of children's cereals, "Cocoa Pebbles", "Fruity Pebbles", "Alpha-Bits", "Sugar Crisp" and "Honeycombs", claiming that the cereals contain 38%-47% sugar, despite being advertised as a *"nutritious breakfast cereal"*. **30**		
"Seattle Slew" wins Belmont to complete horse racing's "Triple Crown". (See June 11th) Jacqueline Bisset and Nick Nolte star in the new film "The Deep". (See June 21st)				"Star Wars" film characters "R2-D2" and "C-3PO" on Owen Lars' homestead on Tatooine. (See June 8th)		

JULY 1977

Tom Watson with caddy Alf Fyles are congratulated by Jack Nicklaus after winning the British Open Golf Title.

Sunday	Monday	Tuesday	Wednesday	Thursday	Friday	Saturday
	Martin Mull stars as host "Barth Gimble" on the new TV program "Fernwood 2-Night". (See July 4th)	 Sweden's Bjorn Borg, 21, captures the Wimbledon Men's Singles Tennis Title. (See July 2nd) American Tom Watson captures the Men's British Open Golf Title at Turnberry. (See July 9th)		 Great Britain's Virginia Wade, 31, defeats Betty Stove 4-6, 6-3, 6-1 to win the **Wimbledon Women's Singles Tennis Title**. Wade is the 1st Englishwoman player to win a singles title here since 1969 when Adrienne Jones defeated American Billie Jean King.	Great Britain's Virginia Wade, 31, defeats Betty Stove 4-6, 6-3, 6-1 to win the **Wimbledon Women's Singles Tennis Title**... A new Broadway play, **"California Suite"** opens in New York City. The Neil Simon play will enjoy a run of 445 performances. **1**	In what will be called one of the greatest tennis matches of all time, Sweden's **Bjorn Borg**, 21, defeats American Jimmy Connors 3-6, 6-2, 6-1, 5-7, 6-4 to win the Wimbledon Men's Singles title. The gruelling final takes 3 hours and 14 minutes before Borg prevails. **2**
Chart Toppers: The #1 pop single is "Gonna Fly Now" (theme from the film Rocky) by Bill Conti. Dave Eichelberger wins the **Greater Milwaukee Golf** Open to take home $26,000. **3**	Americans celebrate the nation's **201st birthday**.  A new syndicated TV program, **"Fernwood 2 Night"**, premieres. Developed by Norman Lear, the show is a satire on talk shows starring Martin Mull as host "Barth Gimble" with Fred Willard as sidekick "Jerry Hubard". **4**	The popularity of **"Happy Days"** on television has led to mass merchandising of "Fonzie" products. Henry Winkler plays "The Fonz", a nonconformist, black-leather-jacket-wearing "cool" character. Fonzie t-shirts, buttons, posters and socks with a picture of "Fonzie" with his thumb pointing up have all become top-sellers. **5**	The **top-grossing films** in the U.S. at this time are: 1) "The Deep" 2) "Star Wars" 3) "Exorcist II - The Heretic" 4) "The Other Side of Midnight" 5) "A Bridge Too Far" The average price for **precious metals** is $148 an ounce of gold and $4.62 for an ounce of silver. **6**	The small town of Matsushiro, about 120 miles northwest of Tokyo, reports that since 1965 there have been **720,665 earthquakes** recorded here although only 63,104 were large enough for humans to detect. The combined energy of all the quakes since 1965 equals only one 6.5 tremor. **7**	The new **Trans-Alaska Pipeline** is shut down after an explosion and fire at pump station No. 8 kills one person and injures five others. The federal government will not allow the flow of oil to continue until an inquiry is completed. The #1 song on the Country and Western chart is **"That Was Yesterday"** by Donna Fargo. **8**	American Tom Watson shoots back-to-back rounds of 65 to win the 106th **British Open** Golf Championship by one stroke over 1966 and 1970 champion Jack Nicklaus on the Turnberry Scotland Golf Course. Watson wins the £10,000 first prize, setting a new British Open record of 268 for 72 holes. In April, Watson also won the Masters to win two majors this year. **9**
According to recent Gallup polls, close to six million Americans are currently practicing **transcendental meditation**. In addition, five million practice yoga, while millions of others experiment with mysticism and other eastern religions. According to recent surveys, 7 out of 10 Americans describe themselves as church members. **10**	**Chart Toppers:** The #1 pop single is "Undercover Angel" by Alan O'Day. The #1 pop album is "Rumours" by Fleetwood Mac. The #1 R & B single is "The Best Of My Love" by The Emotions. The #1 song on the Country and Western chart is **"I'll Be Leaving Alone"** by Charley Pride. **11**	194 protesters are arrested at **Kent State** during a protest against the construction of a gymnasium on the site where 4 students had been killed protesting U.S. war intrusions into Cambodia during 1970. Included in those arrested are the parents of one of the slain students. **12**	An **electrical storm** in New York City causes power failure to 9 million people throughout the five boroughs and Westchester County for between 4 1/2 and 25 hours. Both LaGuardia and Kennedy International Airports are closed for 8 hours as well as banks, stores and the Stock Exchange. Looting and vandalism results in the arrest of 3,700 people. **13**	**The United States Postal Service** is charging customers 13 cents to mail a 1st-class letter anywhere within the country. The U.S. Post Office first began service in 1775, collecting a minimum of 6 cents to deliver a letter less than 30 miles and up to a maximum of 25 cents for more than 450 miles. **14**	Saxophonist Robert De Niro and vocalist Liza Minnelli love and fight with each other right through the big band era in the musical drama film **"New York, New York"** directed by Martin Scorsese. Kathleen Quinlan and Bibi Anderson star in the film **"I Never Promised You A Rose Graden"** directed by Anthony Page. **15**	**Chart Toppers:** The #1 pop single is "Da Roo Ron Ron" by Shaun Cassidy. The #1 song on the Country and Western chart is **"It Was Almost Like a Song"** by Ronnie Milsap. **16**
Comic **Phyllis Diller** celebrates her 60th birthday. Raymond Floyd wins the **Pleasant Valley Golf Classic** at Sutton, Massachusetts, to take home the $50,000 first prize. **17**	**Major League Baseball Standings:** **NL East** - Chicago holds a two-game lead over Philadelphia **NL West** - Los Angeles is 9 1/2 games ahead of Cincinnati **AL East** - Baltimore has a slim 1/2-game lead over Boston **AL West** - Chicago is 2 1/2 games ahead of Kansas City **18**	The 48th Annual Major League Baseball **All-Star game** is won 7-5 by the National League at Yankee Stadium in New York. The senior circuit jumps out to a 4-0 first-inning lead on home runs by Joe Morgan and Greg Luzinski off pitcher Jim Palmer. L.A. Dodgers pitcher Don Sutton gets the win and is also awarded the game MVP honor. The National League now leads the series 29-18-1. **19**	A **flash flood** sweeps through Johnstown, Pennsylvania, along the Conemaugh River Valley, killing 68 people and causing over $200 million in damages. In addition, 31 people are reported as missing. **20**	With gas prices high, **"mopeds"** have become a practical and trendy travel item. More than a bicycle and less than a motorcycle, mopeds get up to 220 miles per gallon of gas. Mopeds range from $295 to $400 and are a very common sight on college campuses around the country. **21**	Burt Reynolds and Kris Kristofferson play two football stars in the comedy film **"Semi-Tough"** with Jill Clayburgh, Robert Preston, Bert Convy, Lotte Lenya, Roger Mosley, Richard Maslir, Carl Weathers and Brian Dennehy. **22**	**Chart Toppers:** The #1 pop single is "Looks Like We Made It" by Barry Manilow. The #1 pop album continues to be "Rumours" by Fleetwood Mac. The #1 United Kingdom pop single is "I Feel Love" by Donna Summer. **23**
Hollis Stacy, 23, led from start to finish to win the 25th **U.S. Women's Open Golf Championship** on the tough Hazeltine National Golf Club in Minnesota, by 2 strokes over Nancy Lopez who is playing in her first professional tournament. Stacy earns $11,000 for the win. Lee Trevino wins the **Canadian Open** golf title at Glen Abbey to take home $45,000. **24**	The first of two **typhoons** named "Thelma" and "Vera" sweep across the island of Taiwan, with winds up to 120 mph, killing 39 people. A killer whale seeks revenge on the crew that killed his pregnant mate in **"ORCA"**, starring Richard Harris, Charlotte Rampling, Will Sampson, Peter Hooten, Bo Derek, Keenan Wynn, and Robert Carradine. The movie is directed by Michael Anderson. **25**	A **fire** burns through the Santa Barbara, California, suburb of Montecito, destroying more than 250 luxurious homes and causing damages estimated over $24 million. More than 3,000 people had to be evacuated from the area which is in the second year of a severe drought. **26**	**Citizens band radio** continues to be one of the hottest fads in the country. The craze first began in 1973 when there was an oil embargo and a truckers' strike. Many Americans purchased a CB as an efficient way of finding an open gas station or as a way to avoid police radar or traffic congestion. Over 3 million Americans now have a CB licence. **27**	A truck carrying $3.54 million in newly minted coins is **hijacked** in Paris by armed gunmen who escape with 17 tons of coins in the "heaviest holdup ever in the world". **28**	Crude oil arrives in Valdez after a 38-day stretch during which the **Trans-Alaska Pipeline** was shut down six times. The pipeline is capable of transporting 1.2 million barrels of oil each day. The "S.S. Arco Juneau" will be the first tanker loaded and will arrive at Cherry Point, Washington, on August 5th. **29**	Roger Moore stars as "007 James Bond" (for the third time) in **"The Spy Who Loved Me"** with Barbara Bach, Curt Jurgens, Caroline Munro, Bernard Lee, Lois Maxwell, Desmond Llewellyn and 7'2" Richard Kiel as a persistent steel-toothed goon. Directed by Lewis Gilbert, Carly Simon sings Marvin Hamlisch's theme song "Nobody Does It Better". **30**
Stacy Moscowitz, 20, is murdered and her date partially blinded when they become the latest victims of the **"Son of Sam"** killer who has now murdered six people in New York since July 1976. **31**			Hollis Stacy celebrates her two-stroke victory at the Women's U.S. Open Golf Championship in Minnesota. (See July 24th)	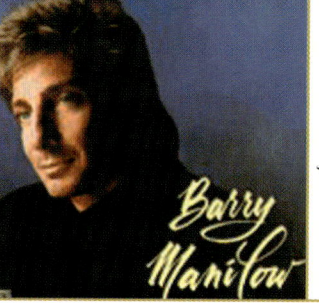	Munsingwear Grand Slam Tenniswear: Shirts $10 Shorts $12 Barry Manilow tops the Pop Singles Music Chart with his hit "Looks Like We Made It". (See July 23rd)	

AUGUST 1977

The world mourns the death of "The King" Elvis Presley.

Sunday	Monday	Tuesday	Wednesday	Thursday	Friday	Saturday
	Soap Box Derby winner (August 20th) Steve Washburn with his parents. Ballantine Books publishes **"Elvis: What Happened?"** by Steve Dunleavy, describing Presley's life in detail, including his extensive drug problems. It is rumored that Elvis seriously considered having Mike Stone, a karate instructor involved with ex-wife Priscilla, killed. Three former bodyguards, Red West, Dave Hebler and Sonny West, were interviewed by Dunleavy for his book. **1**	President Carter endorses legislation that would impose a civil penalty instead of a criminal penalty for possession of **an ounce or less of marijuana** saying "We can and should continue to discourage the use of marijuana without defining the smoker as a criminal". **2**	The hottest hairstyle for girls is the new **"Farrah Fawcett"** look. Last year, the Dorothy Hamill cut was the trend but, sparked by the star of the hit TV show "Charlie's Angels", long flowing hair is back in vogue. In addition to the hair, Farrah Fawcett t-shirts and posters are also very popular. **3**	The popularity of the hit movie **"Star Wars"**, directed by George Lucas, has led to millions of $1 buttons that read "May The Force Be With You" being worn by fans of the sci-fi futuristic adventure. Other popular products are Darth Vader posters, Star Wars key chains for $1.50 and necklaces for $1. **4**	Part of a massive **energy bill** passed by the House calls for so-called *gas-guzzler cars* to be taxed beginning in 1979. The **Exxon Corporation** marks its 95th anniversary. **5**	Former NY Jet quarterback, **Joe Namath** makes his debut with the L.A. Rams in a pre-season game against visiting Minnesota Vikings. Pop artist **Andy Warhol** celebrates his 50th birthday. **6**
Chart Toppers: The #1 pop single is "I Just Want To Be Your Everything" by Andy Gibb. The #1 pop album is once again "Rumours" by Fleetwood Mac. The #1 R & B single is "Strawberry Letter 23" by The Brothers Johnson. Bill Kratzert, 25, earns $42,000 as he captures his 1st PGA tour title at the **Greater Hartford** golf event. **7**	Demolition begins of a black shantytown where 11,000 people live outside **Cape Town**, South Africa. Police use tear gas to clear both black and white demonstrators. Actor **Dustin Hoffman** celebrates his 40th birthday. **8**	The NHL Board of Governors votes **to reject a proposed merger** with the World Hockey Association for the 1977-1978 season. The #1 song on the Country and Western chart is **"Rollin' With the Flow"** by Charlie Rich. **9**	One of the most dramatic manhunts in the nation's history ends as New York City police arrest **David Richard Berkowitz**, 24, in connection with the string of "Son of Sam" murders. Berkowitz is charged with second-degree murder for the shooting death of Stacy Moskowitz, aged 20, that occurred on July 31st. **10**	Cuban President **Fidel Castro** allows some 80 U.S. citizens to leave Cuba with their Cuban-born wives and children. **Rick Nelson** is awarded a gold record for his hit single "Travelin' Man". **11**	The reusable space shuttle **"Enterprise"** makes its first test flight. The shuttle is carried on a Boeing 747 and released. It glides on its own for five and one half minutes, landing safely in the Mojave Desert near Edwards Air Force Base. Fred Haise and C. Gordon Fullerton piloted the craft. CBS-TV premieres a musical variety **"The Keane Brothers Show"** hosted by Tom, 12, and John, 13. **12**	A 1/2 gallon of fresh milk is selling at an average price of 84¢ in supermarkets across the country. ABC-TV premieres a rock-and-roll sitcom, **"Sugar Time"**, about a trio called "Sugar". The program stars Barbi Benton as "Maxx", Marianne Black as "Maggie" and Didi Carr as "Diane". **13**
The 59th Professional Golf Championship is won by **Lanny Wadkins** on the 3rd sudden-death play-off hole at the Pebble Beach Golf links in California. Wadkins won the play-off over Gene Littler who had tied with Wadkins at 282 after 72 holes. **14**	The largest crowd ever to see a **soccer** game in the U.S. or Canada, 77,691 fans watch a NASL play-off game at Giants Stadium in East Rutherford, New Jersey, home of the Cosmos. The Cosmos are led by Franz Beckenbauer, Pele (Edson Arantes do Nascimento), Steve Hunt, Giorgio Chinaglia and Shep Messing. **15**	**Elvis Presley**, the King of Rock and Roll, dies in Memphis at the age of 42 of a suspected cardiac arrest. Elvis' many hits include "Jailhouse Rock", "Hound Dog", and "Love Me Tender". Presley's songs sold over 500 million records. During his career, Elvis had 28 gold records and also appeared in numerous films. **16**	The New York State Supreme Court rules that the U.S. Tennis Association could not legally prevent transsexual **Dr. Renee Richards** from playing in the upcoming Women's U.S. Open. The Russia news agency TASS has reported that the nuclear-powered icebreaker **"Arktika"** has become the first surface vessel in history to reach the North Pole. **17**	Some 75,000 fans mourn the death of **Elvis Presley** as he is buried at the Forest Hill Cemetery in Memphis, Tennessee, near the grave of his mother Gladys who also died at the age of 42. Actor **Robert Redford** celebrates his 40th birthday. **18**	The nation's most important outdoor swimming competition, the AAU National Long-Course Championships take place in Mission Viejo, California, between athletes from the U.S., Australia, Canada, South Africa and other countries. The U.S. women's team sets one world record by Alice Browe in the 1500m freestyle and seven U.S. records, winning 12 of their 15 events over the 4-day event. **19**	Mark Ferdinand, 10, of Canton, Ohio, (junior) and Steve Washburn of Bristol, Connecticut, (senior) capture the 40th Annual All-American **Soap Box Derby** Championships in Akron, Ohio. **Groucho Marx**, 86, dies of pneumonia in Los Angeles. The zany cigar-smoking comedian was considered by many as the main member of The Marx Brothers comedy team. **20**
Chart Toppers: The #1 pop single is "Best Of My Life" by The Emotions. The #1 pop album is "Rumours" by Fleetwood Mac for the 17th week in a row. The #1 song on the Country and Western chart is **"Way Down"** by Elvis Presley. **21**	**Elvis Presley** fans buy up a 16-page rotogravure magazine section in the Louisville, Kentucky, "Courier-Journal", driving circulation to a record 385,000. By August 24th, 6.5 million copies will be sold. RCA Records' Indianapolis plant is working 24 hours a day producing 250,000 albums and 200,000 singles each day. The largest single book order in history (more than 2 million copies) is "Elvis: What Happened?" by Steve Dunleavy. **22**	British-born actor **Sebastian Cabot**, 59, dies in Victoria, British Columbia. Cabot is best remembered for his roles in the TV series "Checkmate" (1960-1962) as "Carl Hyatt", and "Family Affair" (1966-1969) as "Mr. Giles French". **23**	According to the Bureau of Land Management, more than 8,600 **fires** since the beginning of the year have burned nearly 400,000 acres of national forests in one of the worst fire seasons in history. **24**	The engagement of **Princess Caroline** of Monaco, 20, (daughter of Prince Ranier and former Hollywood movie star Grace Kelly) to Philippe Jundt, 37, is announced. **25**	Cecil Browne catches a **world record** Atlantic Bigeye Tuna weighing 375 lbs, 8 oz in waters off the coast of Ocean City, Maryland. An historic and controversial law **"that limits the use of English"** in the province of Quebec, Canada, Bill 101 is passed in the Quebec National Assembly. **26**	The 31st Annual **Little League** World Series of Baseball at Williamsport, Pennsylvania, is won by Taipei of Taiwan 7-2 over El Cajon of California. Pitcher Chiang Chen-Jung went 8-0 in the tournament and batted .833 in 12 at bats. The N.Y. Apples defend their World Team Tennis Title with a 28-17 win over the Phoenix Racquets in Phoenix. **27**
Soccer Bowl '77 is won by the Cosmos who capture their second North American Soccer League Championship with a 2-1 win over the Seattle Sounders at Portland's Civic Stadium. Steve Hunt, a 21-year-old Englishman, scores the first goal, assists on the second and is named as the game's MVP. **28**	St. Louis Cardinal outfielder **Lou Brock**, 38, steals two bases in a game against the San Diego Padres in San Diego, to tie and break the Major League Baseball base-stealing record held by Hall-of-Famer Ty Cobb who, between 1905-1928 with the Detroit Tigers and Philadelphia Athletics, stole 892 bases. **29**	The #1 song on the Country and Western chart is **"Don't It Make My Brown Eyes Blue"** by Crystal Gayle. The hit song will remain on the top of the country chart until September 24th when Conway Twitty's hit "I've Already Loved You In My Mind" will take over the top spot. **30**	The **top-grossing films** in the U.S. at this time are: 1) Star Wars 2) One On One 3) Bad News Bears in Breaking Training 4) The Spy Who Loved Me 5) Kentucky Fried Movie **31**	St. Louis Cardinal Lou Brock breaks Ty Cobb's record of 829 stolen bases with his steal of 2nd base during the 7th inning. (See August 29th)		

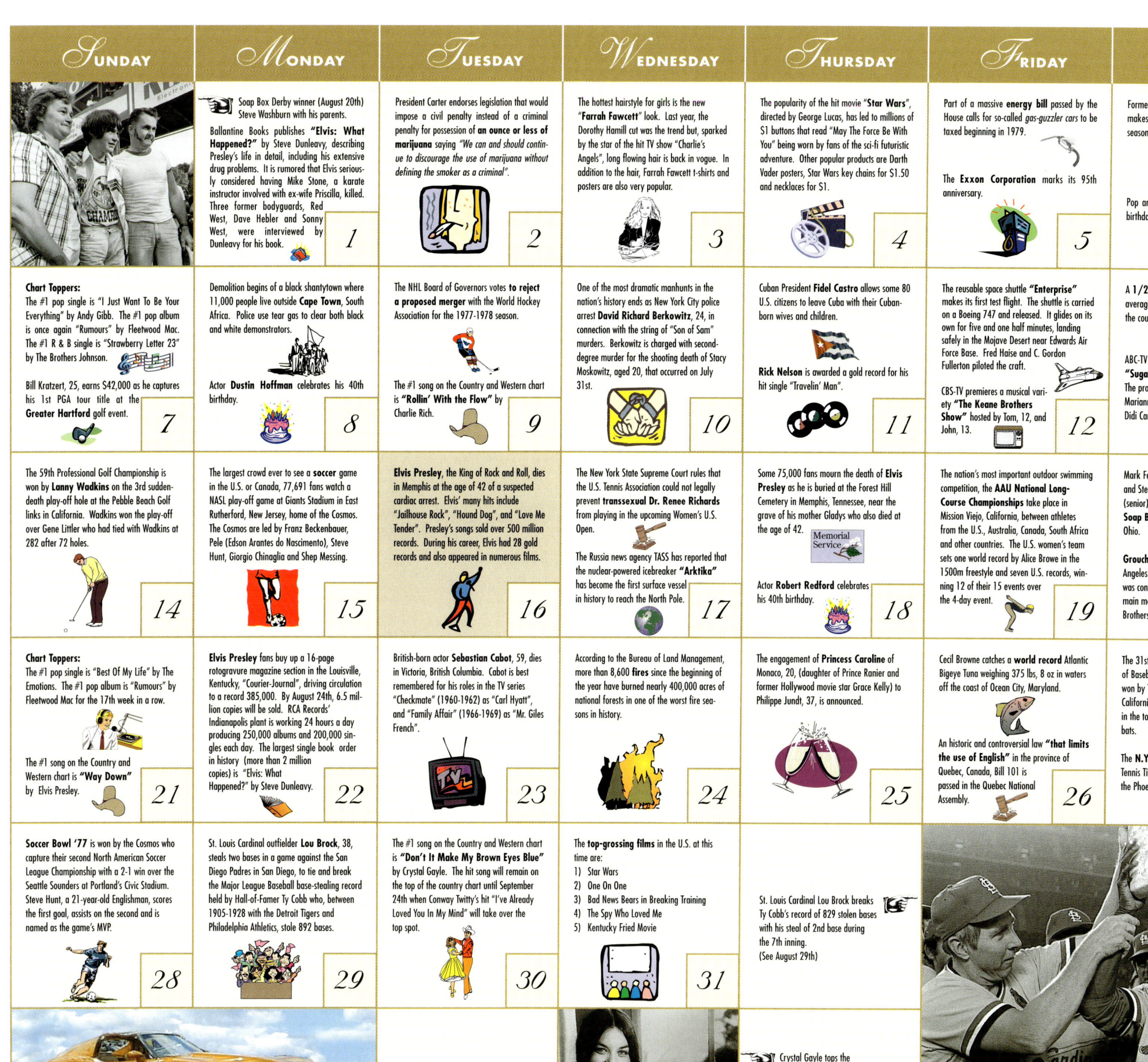

1977 Chevrolet Corvette

Crystal Gayle tops the Country and Western Music chart with her hit song "Don't It Make My Brown Eyes Blue". (See August 30th)

SEPTEMBER 1977

ABC-TV premieres the new comedy series "Soap".

Sunday	Monday	Tuesday	Wednesday	Thursday	Friday	Saturday

Larry Wilcox and Eric Estrada star in the new TV series "CHIPS". (See September 15th)

ABC-TV premieres the new TV series "The Love Boat". (See September 24th)

1 — The Top Five Songs on the Pop Music Chart at this time are:
(1) "Best Of My Love" by The Emotions
(2) "I Just Want To Be Your Everything" by Andy Gibb
(3) "(Your Love Has Lifted Me) Higher and Higher" by Rita Coolidge
(4) "I'm In You" by Peter Frampton
(5) "Easy" by The Commodores

2 — Hershey Foods, makers of fine chocolate bars since 1895, introduces **"Golden Almond"**, a new candy bar.

3 — Tokyo's Yomiuri Giants first baseman, **Sadaharli Oh** becomes the most prolific home-run hitter in professional baseball, hitting his 756th home run off pitcher Yasumiro Suzuki of the Yakult Swallows at Tokyo's Korakuen Stadium, surpassing Major League Baseball's Hank Aaron who retired in 1976 with 755 round-trippers.

Way To Go!

4 — The smash Broadway play **"Godspell"**, a rock musical by Stephen Schwartz, plays for the last time at Cherry Lane Theater after 527 performances and after having played previously for 2,118 showings off Broadway. The musical will long be associated with the hit song "Day By Day" that was introduced during 1972.

BROADWAY

5 — The 77th **U.S. National Amateur Golf Championship** is won by John Fought over Doug Fischesser 9 & 8 at the Aronmink Golf Club in Pennsylvania.

CBS-TV premieres a medical drama **"Rafferty"**, starring Patrick McGoohan as "Dr. Sidney Rafferty". The network also premieres **"The Fitzpatricks"**, a drama about a middle-class family with a dog named "Detroit".

6 — Canada begins to convert highway speed limit and distance signs to the **metric system**, following the 1975 conversion of temperatures to Celsius scale from Fahrenheit.

SPEED LIMIT 55

Following yesterday's successful launch, the unmanned space probe **"Voyager I"** is speeding toward Jupiter and Saturn.

7 — A new **Panama Canal** treaty is signed by President Carter and Panama's Chief of Government Brig Gen Omar Torrijos in Washington. The U.S. will operate the canal until December 31st, 1999, when Panama will take control.

The youngest player ever to appear in a U.S. Open tennis match, **Tracy Austin**, 14, loses in the quarter-finals to Betty Stove.

8 — Canadian marathon swimmer **Cindy Nicholas**, 20, becomes the first female to swim the English Channel nonstop both ways, knocking an incredible ten hours and 5 minutes off the men's record.

9 — The best-selling mass market **paperback books** in the U.S. at this time are:
1) "Passages" by Gail Sheehy
2) "Star Wars" by George Lucas
3) "Touch Not The Cat" by Mary Stewart
4) "The Other Side of Midnight" by Sidney Sheldon
5) "Ordinary People" by Judith Guest

10 — NBC-TV premieres a new cartoon show, **"I Am The Greatest - The Adventures Of Muhammad Ali"** which features the real voice of Ali.

Miss Ohio, Susan Perkins, 23, is selected as the new **Miss America** in Atlantic City. Perkins is the 5th winner from the state of Ohio.

11 — The 29th Annual Television **Emmy Awards** are presented to the following:
Outstanding Limited Series: "Roots"
Actor Drama Series: James Garner "The Rockford Files"
Actress Drama Series: Lindsay Wagner "The Bionic Woman"
Actor Comedy Series: Carroll O'Connor "All In The Family"
Actress Comedy Series: Beatrice Arthur "Maude"

12 — One of the most influential black student leaders in South Africa, **Steven Biko** is reported to have died from a hunger strike he began while in police detention on Sept. 5th. Biko was the founder of the South African students organization and co-founder with Kenneth Rachidi of the Black People's Convention.

CBS-TV premieres **"The Betty White Show"** starring White as "Joyce Whitman".

13 — ABC-TV premieres a new prime-time comedy serial, **"Soap"**, that revolves around 2 families "The Tates" and "The Campbell's" who reside in Dunn River, Connecticut. Created, produced, and written by Susan Harris ,the controversial program has a large cast of characters which includes Billy Crystal "Jodie", Katherine Helmond "Jessica" and Robert Mandan "Chester".

14 — President Carter declares Missouri as a **disaster area** after Kansas City was hit with a flash flood when 12 inches of rain fell over a 24-hour period, killing 26 people. The downtown Country Club Plaza Hotel and Shopping Complex is the hardest hit as up to six feet of water poured into its stores and restaurants.

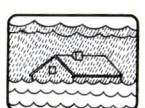

15 — NBC-TV premieres a new action police program, **"CHIPS"** (California Highway Patrol), starring Eric Estrada as "Poncho" and Larry Wilcox as "Jonathan", two motorcycle patrol cops.

ABC-TV premieres **"The Redd Foxx Comedy Hour"** starring the former "Sanford and Son" star comic.

16 — NBC-TV premieres **"The Sanford Arms"** in an effort to keep "Sanford and Son's" popularity going, despite the departures of Redd Foxx and Demond Wilson. The new program stars Teddy Wilson as the bar's new owner "Phil".

Consumers purchasing a loaf of **white bread** are paying an average price of 35¢ at supermarkets across the nation.

17 — The U.S., led by non-playing captain Dow Finsterwald, wins the 22nd **Ryder Cup** Golf Challenge matches over Great Britain 12 1/2 to 7 1/2 on the Royal Lytham and St. Anne's Course in England. The U.S. now leads 18 cups to 3 with 1 tie.

ABC-TV premieres **"Operation Petticoat"**, a show about a group of army nurses aboard a submarine during WWII.

18 — The U.S. yacht "Courageous", skippered by Ted Turner, successfully defends the **Americas Cup**, winning 4 races to none in waters off the coast of Newport, Rhode Island, over the Australian challenger "Australia", skippered by Noel Robins. This is the 23rd Challenge Race here since 1870, all of which have been won by the American squads.

19 — Movie director **Roman Polanski**, who pleaded guilty to unlawful sexual intercourse with a 13-year-old girl, is ordered imprisoned for 90 days for psychiatric examination. The incarceration, however, will be delayed for 3 months as Polanski is working in Tahiti on a film.

Director

20 — **Christina Onassis**, daughter of deceased Aristotle Onassis, has offered her stepmother, Jacqueline Kennedy Onassis, a $20-million settlement to end all claims on his estate.

The U.S. and Canada sign a agreement to construct a 3,500-mile **Pipeline** to carry Alaskan natural gas across Canada to the lower U.S.

CBS-TV premieres **"Lou Grant"** starring Ed Asner.

21 — President Carter announces to the nation the resignation of Budget Director, **Bert Lance**, following a lengthy and ongoing controversy centered around Lance's personal financial dealings.

22 — The third and last ***no-hitter*** of this season in Major League Baseball is registered by right-hander Bert Blyleven, 26, of the Texas Rangers, as he hurls a superb no-hit 9-0 shutout over the home-field California Angels in an American League contest. There have been 3 *no-hitters* registered so far during the 1976 season.

23 — The **Dow Jones** closes on the New York Stock Exchange at 839.14, down from 876.39 on September 7th, its lowest close since December 22th, 1975.

WALL ST.

24 — ABC-TV premieres a new series, **"The Love Boat"**, which features guests in vignettes aboard a cruise ship "The Pacific Princess". The regular crew members aboard the ship include Gavin MacLeod "Captain Stubing", Bernie Koppell "Doc", Ted Lange "Isaac" and Lauren Tewes as "Julie" the cruise-director.

25 — The EPA rates the diesel engine **Volkswagen Rabbit** as the top fuel economy car on the market, with an average of 45 miles a gallon for city and highway driving. The Oldsmobile diesel-powered Delta 88 and 98 were top-rated in fuel economy among the 8-cylinder models.

26 — **Chart Toppers:**
The #1 pop single is "Best Of My Love" by The Emotions for the sixth straight week. The #1 pop album is "Rumours" by Fleetwood Mac for the 19th straight week.

27 — Consumer advocate **Ralph Nader** announces plans to form a group to defend the interests of the country's sports fans called FANS (Fight To Advance The Nation's Sports).

The #1 song on the Country and Western chart is **"I've Already Loved You in My Mind"** by Conway Twitty.

28 — Sophia Loren and Marcello Mastroianni star as two lonely people who meet by chance on an eventful day in 1938 in the Italian-Canadian film **"A Special Day"**, directed by Ettore Scola.

ADMIT ONE

29 — World Heavyweight Champion, **Muhammad Ali**, 35, retains his title for the 10th time when he wins a 15-round unanimous decision over Ernie Shavers, 33, during their bout in New York City. Eva Shain becomes the first woman to judge in a world heavyweight title fight.

30 — General Motors has introduced the first **diesel-powered** car manufactured by a U.S. auto maker. Oldsmobile Delta 88 and 98 models are priced an average of $850 more than regular engine models. According to EPA tests, they are 40% more fuel efficient than their gasoline powered counterparts.

Skipper Ted Turner and his crew celebrate their America's Cup Victory by jumping into the Newport Harbor. (See September 18th)

"Major Charles Emerson Winchester III" (David Ogden Stiers) joins the cast of M*A*S*H during a one-hour special marking the start of the series 6th season on September 20th.

OCTOBER 1977

New York Yankees – 1977 World Series Champions

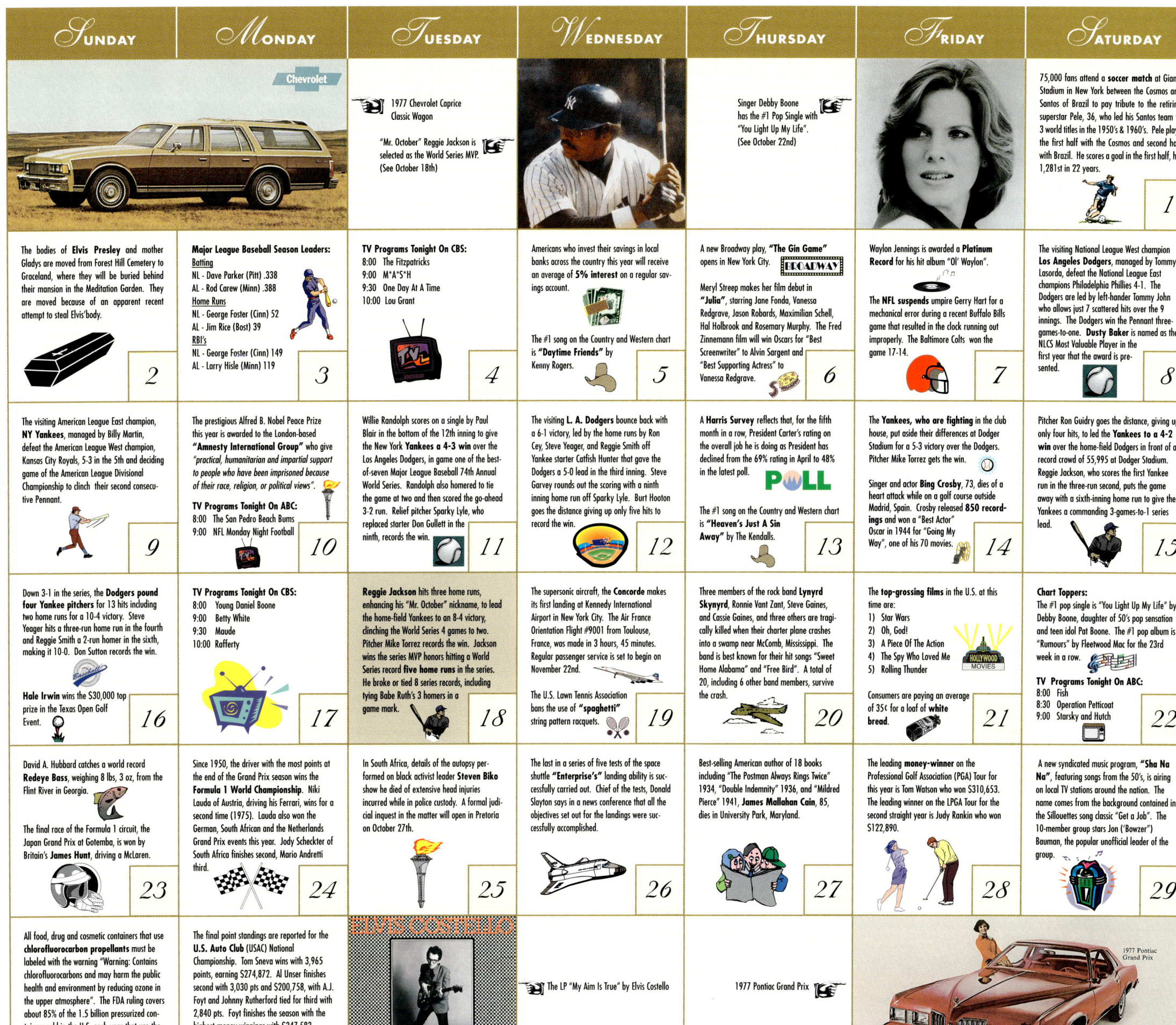

NOVEMBER *1977*

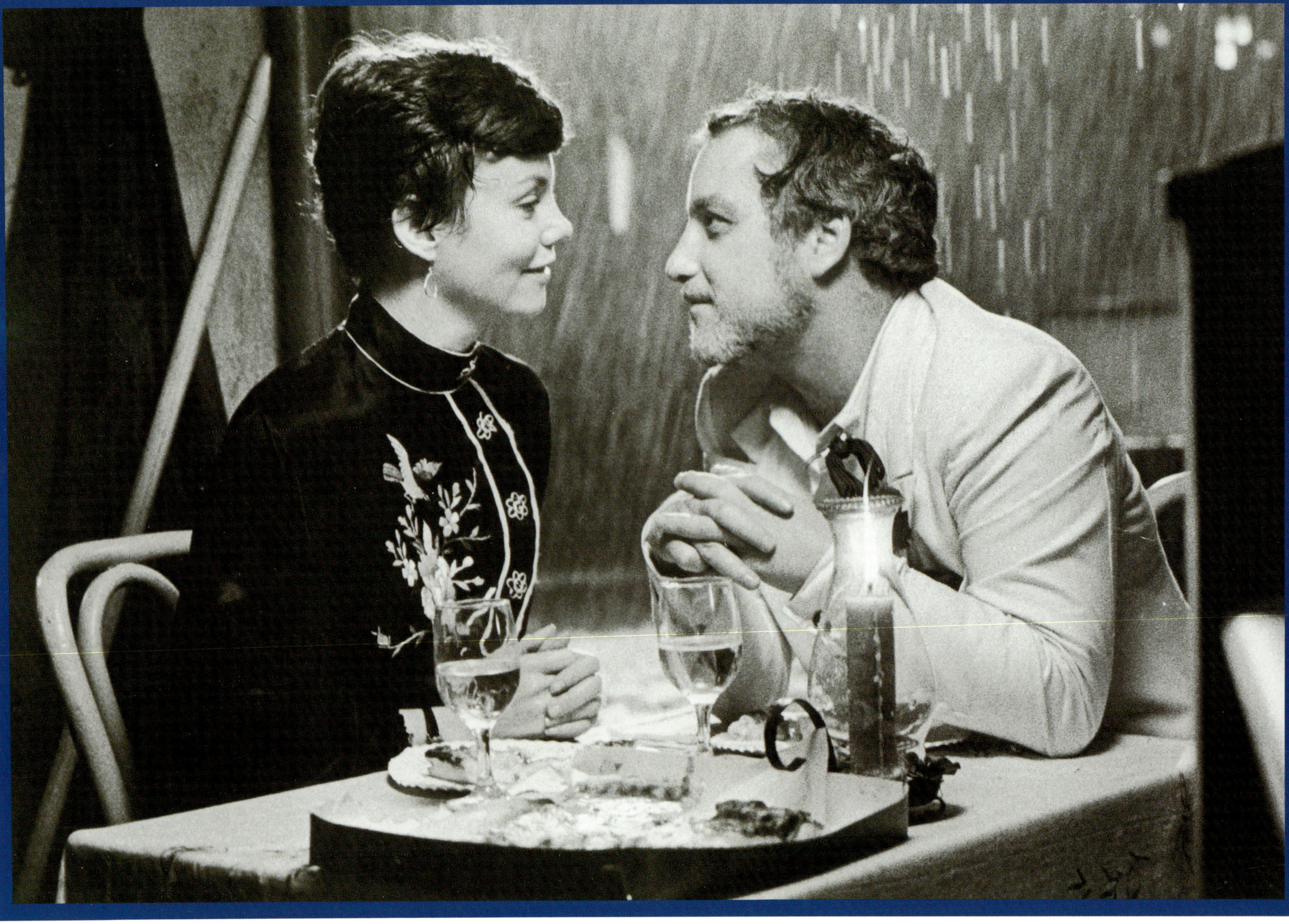

Marsha Mason and Richard Dreyfuss star in the new film "The Goodbye Girl".

Sunday	Monday	Tuesday	Wednesday	Thursday	Friday	Saturday

1 — Jaclyn Smith and Kate Jackson with new angel Cheryl Ladd star in the hit TV adventure series "Charlie's Angels". (See November 9th)

The Federal Drug Enforcement Administration (DEA) reports that the veterinary tranquilizer called **phencyclidine** (PCP) has become a popular drug among teenagers which can cause serious health hazards.

2 — The **Cy Young Memorial Award** presented annually since 1956 to MLB's best pitchers goes to American League NY Yankee Sparky Lyle and to the National League Philadelphia Phillie Steve Carleton, who also won the award in 1972.

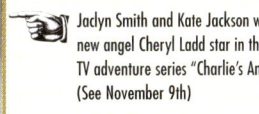

3 — **Francine Hughes**, 30, charged with first-degree murder in the death of her husband, is found **not guilty** by reason of temporary insanity. Mrs. Hughes had been beaten, choked and threatened by her husband before she poured gasoline under his bed and set the house on fire. The story will become the subject of a much-publicized motion picture.

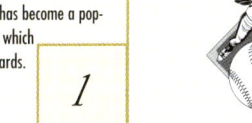

4 — **"Beatlomania"** is a nostalgic review of the early 1960's as portrayed by four Beatles look-alike actors who take the show to Broadway for 1,006 performances at the Winter Garden Theater. It will close in 1980 before a similar show by the same name will appear.

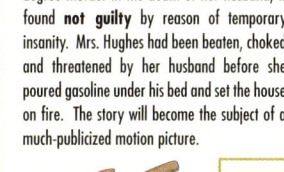

BROADWAY

5 — Rodrigo Valdes of Colombia wins the **World Middleweight Boxing Title** (vacated by retired Carlos Monzon of Argentina) with a unanimous 15-round decision over American Bennie Briscoe in Italy.

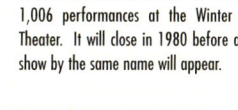

Ken Norton emerges as the #1 heavyweight contender with a 15-round split decision over Jimmy Young at Caesar's Palace in Las Vegas.

6 — The 26-foot-high **Kelley Barnes Dam** in northeastern Georgia bursts, sending more than **112 million gallons** of water 800 feet below, killing 39 people on the campus of Toccoa Falls Bible College. An additional 45 others are injured in the tragedy.

7 — The best-selling **fiction books** in the U.S. at this time are:

1) "The Simarillion" by J.R.R. Tolkien
2) "The Thorn Birds" by Colleen McCullough
3) "The Honourable Schoolboy" by John LeCarré

The #1 song on the Country and Western chart is **"I'm Just a Country Boy"** by Don Williams.

8 — **Edward I. Koch** (D) becomes the 105th Mayor of New York City, winning 50% of the total vote in a four-way race, edging out his closest opponent Mario Cuomo. On the winning ticket is State Senator Carol Bellamy who becomes N.Y.'s **first woman elected** to office as City Council President.

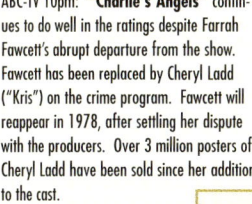

9 — ABC-TV 10pm: **"Charlie's Angels"** continues to do well in the ratings despite Farrah Fawcett's abrupt departure from the show. Fawcett has been replaced by Cheryl Ladd ("Kris") on the crime program. Fawcett will reappear in 1978, after settling her dispute with the producers. Over 3 million posters of Cheryl Ladd have been sold since her addition to the cast.

10 — **The Johnson & Johnson Corporation** celebrates its 90th Anniversary.

Happy Anniversary

TV Programs Tonight On ABC:

8:00 Welcome Back, Kotter
8:30 What's Happening!!
9:00 Barney Miller
9:30 Carter Country
10:00 Redd Foxx Comedy Hour

11 — In his first starring film role, Henry Winkler plays a crazy Vietnam veteran who chases his dream of fame and fortune in **"Heroes"**, co-starring Sally Field and Harrison Ford.

TV Programs Tonight On NBC:

8:00 Sanford Arms
8:30 Chico and The Man
9:00 The Rockford Files
10:00 Quincy

12 — **Ernest N. Morial**, 48, is elected Mayor of New Orleans, becoming the city's first black mayor. Morial was also the first black to graduate from Louisiana State University, the first black elected since reconstruction to the Louisiana House of Representatives, and the first black elected to the Louisiana Appeals Court.

13 — **Chart Toppers:**
The #1 pop single for the fifth week in a row is the Platinum hit "You Light Up My Life" by Debby Boone. The #1 pop album is "Rumours" by Fleetwood Mac for the **26th straight record-setting week.**

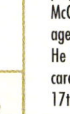

#1

The #1 song on the Country and Western chart is **"More to Me"** by Charley Pride.

14 — Willey McCovey, 39, of the San Francisco Giants becomes the 13th recipient of baseball's **Hutch Award**, named after the late Cincinnati manager Fred Hutchinson who died of cancer in 1964. The award goes to the MLB player who excels despite great adversity. McCovey was passed up in the 1976 free-agent draft because of his age and bad knees. He hit .280 with 86 RBI's, passing the 2,000 career-hit mark, and hit a record 17th career grand slam.

15 — Shah Mohammed Riza Pahlevi of Iran and President Jimmy Carter meet for talks at the White House. Among the topics discussed are **Iran's human rights policies** and the U.S.' views on selling nuclear power plants to Iran.

16 — Singer **Anita Bryant** will have her $100,000-a-year advertising contract with the Florida Citrus Commission renewed until 1979, despite recent boycotts by several gay rights groups protesting Bryant's active stand against homosexuals.

TV Programs Tonight On ABC:

8:00 Eight is Enough
9:00 Charlie's Angels
10:00 Baretta

17 — The Major League Baseball **Most Valuable Player Awards** for this season:
American League award goes to Minnesota Twins first-baseman **Rod Carew** who received 273 points. National League honors go to Cincinnati Reds outfielder **George Foster** who received 291 points.

18 — A 73-year-old retired auto mechanic Robert Edward Chambliss is convicted of first-degree murder in connection with the 1963 bombing of the **16th Street Baptist Church** in Birmingham, Alabama, that killed 4 young black girls and injured other Sunday worshippers in one of the worst acts of racial terrorism during the 1960's civil rights era.

19 — An **historic journey** begins as Egyptian President Anwar Sadat travels to Jerusalem at the invitation of Israeli Prime Minister Menachem Begin. This is the first time since the creation of Israel in 1948 that an Egyptian leader has met with an Israeli leader on Israeli soil. Other Arab states see Sadat's visit as improper and condemn the visit.

20 — NFL Chicago Bears RB **Walter Payton** rushes for 275 yards in a 10-7 victory over the visiting Minnesota Vikings, surpassing the single-game rushing record of 273 yards set by O.J. Simpson in 1976.

Cale Yarborough, the first driver to finish all 30 races he started, wins NASCAR's Winston Cup. He is also the leading money-winner with 9 Grand National event wins.

21 — Richard Dreyfuss struggles with a frustrating enigma that finally comes clean in the Steven Spielberg sci-fi film **"Close Encounters Of The Third Kind"**, with Francois Truffaut, Teri Garr, Melinda Dillon, Cary Guffey and Bob Balaban. The movie is released by Columbia.

22 — The **Concorde** supersonic transport begins its regular passenger service into Kennedy International Airport in New York City from Paris and London. The aircraft can cross the Atlantic Ocean in just 3 1/2 hours.

The #1 song on the Country and Western chart is **"The Wurlitzer Prize (I Don't Want to Get Over You)"** by Waylon Jennings.

23 — The Baseball Writers Association announces outfielder Andrew Dawson, 22, of the Montreal Expos, and designated hitter Eddie Murray, 21, of the Baltimore Orioles, as the National and American League **"Rookies Of The Year"** for major league baseball.

24 — Diane Keaton stars in the film adaptation of Judith Rossner's novel **"Looking For Mr. Goodbar"**, also starring Richard Gere, William Atherton, Tuesday Weld, Richard Kiley, Brian Dennehy, LeVar Burton and Tom Berenger. The movie is directed by Richard Brooks.

ADMIT ONE

25 — American tennis star Jimmy Connors becomes the **men's top prize-money winner** for the fourth consecutive year, winning $922,657 in prize money. Chris Evert is the women's top money-winner, also for the fourth consecutive year, winning $503,134.

26 — Richard Dreyfuss and Marsha Mason star as two lovers in the new film "The Goodbye Girl", scripted by Neil Simon. Directed by Herbert Ross and produced by Ray Stark, the movie also stars Quinn Cummings, Paul Benedict, Barbara Rhoades and Theresa Merritt. Richard Dreyfuss will win a "Best Actor" Oscar for his role in this Warner Brothers film release.

27 — **TV Programs Tonight On CBS:**

7:00 60 Minutes
8:00 Rhoda
8:30 On Our Own
9:00 All In The Family
9:30 Alice
10:00 Kojak

28 — **Chart Toppers:**
The #1 pop single is "You Light Up My Life" by Debby Boone for the 7th week in a row. The #1 pop album for its final week is "Rumours" by Fleetwood Mac.

TV Programs Tonight On CBS:

8:00 Young Daniel Boone
9:00 Betty White
9:30 Maude
10:00 Rafferty

29 — **Tom Ferguson** has won the Professional Rodeo All-Around Championship for the 4th year in a row, having earned $76,730 during this year on the pro circuit.

A new syndicated TV program, **"Second City TV"**, is now airing on stations around the nation. The satire stars John Candy, Andrea Martin, Joe Flaherty, Catherine O'Hara, Dave Thomas and Harold Ramis.

30 — The average cost for an American family to **purchase a home** is $49,600.

According to A. C. Nielson, the **top 5 TV shows** are:

1) Laverne and Shirley
2) Happy Days
3) Three's Company
4) 60 Minutes
5) Charlie's Angels

Vernon Presley, Elvis' father places a rose on his son's grave on November 24th. The press is permitted inside the grounds at "Graceland" for the first time since the death of his son on August 16th.

Alien Spaceships arrive at earth in the new hit film "Close Encounters Of The Third Kind". (See November 21st)

DECEMBER *1977*

Karen Lynn Gorney and John Travolta star in the new film "Saturday Night Fever".

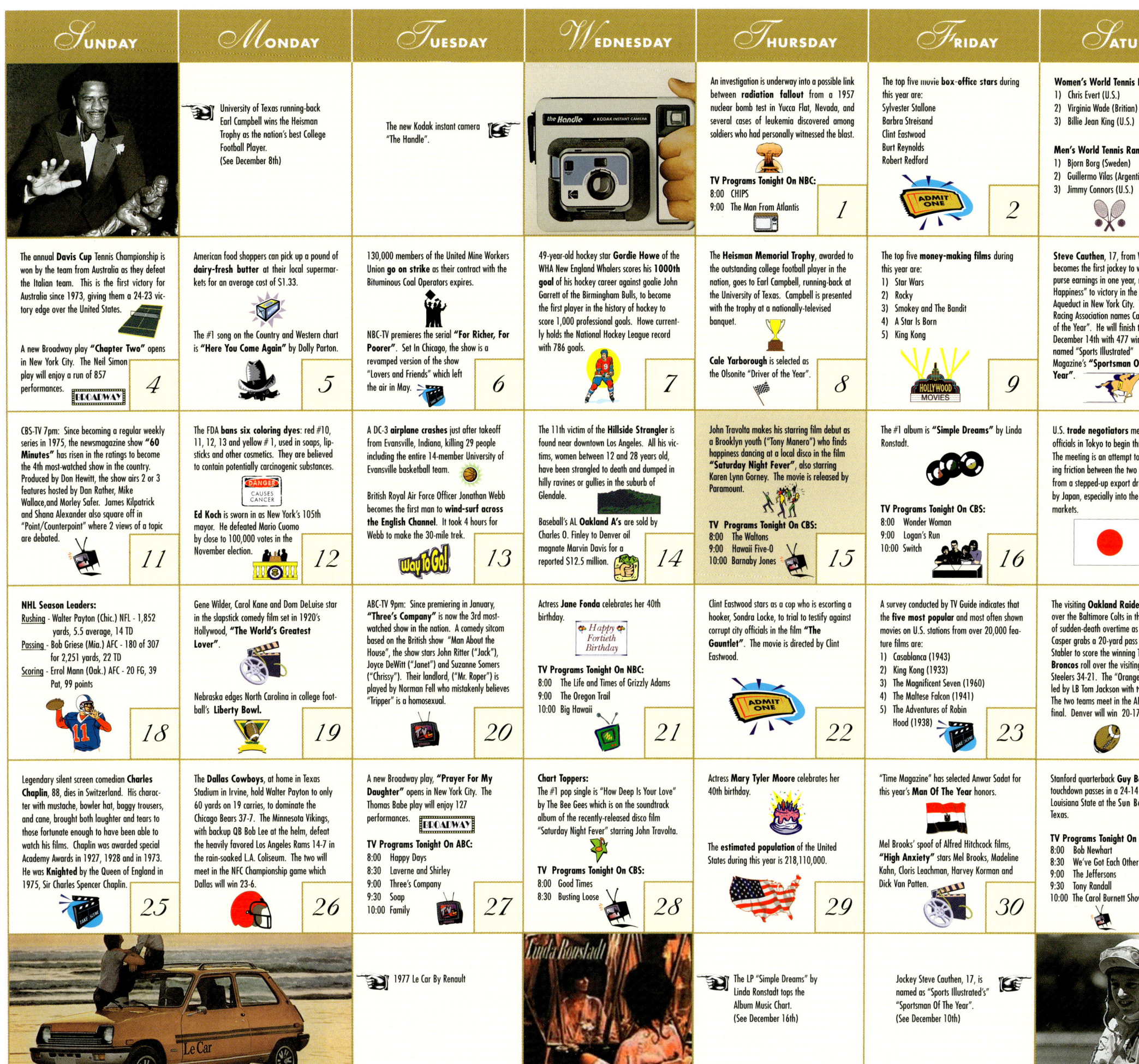